THE JOB OF THE FEDERAL EXECUTIVE

THE JOB
OF THE FEDERAL
EXECUTIVE

by
MARVER H. BERNSTEIN

THE BROOKINGS INSTITUTION
Washington, D.C.

Quotations from " 'Help Wanted' Sign Out . . . Government Gets Few
Takers" are from a copyrighted article in *U. S. News & World Report.*

Quotations from "The Businessman in Government" and "The Little Oscars
and Civil Service" by John McDonald are copyrighted by *Time Inc.*

Quotations from "It Looked Easier on the Outside" by George M. Humphrey with James C. Derieux are reprinted by permission of Mr. Derieux.

Quotations from "To Get Better Men for a Better Government," by John J.
Corson and "Help Wanted: Top Men for Washington," by Jay Walz are
reprinted by permission of the *New York Times.*

Library of Congress Catalogue Card entry appears on page 243

Printed in the United States of America
The George Banta Company, Inc.
Menasha, Wisconsin

THE BROOKINGS INSTITUTION is an independent organization engaged in research and education in the social sciences. Its principal purposes are to aid in the development of sound public policies and to provide advanced training for students in the social sciences.

The Institution was founded December 8, 1927, as a consolidation of three antecedent organizations: the Institute for Government Research, 1916; the Institute of Economics, 1922; and the Robert Brookings Graduate School of Economics and Government, 1924.

The general administration of the Institution is the responsibility of a self-perpetuating Board of Trustees. In addition to this general responsibility the By-Laws provide that, "It is the function of the Trustees to make possible the conduct of scientific research and publication, under the most favorable conditions, and to safeguard the independence of the research staff in the pursuit of their studies and in the publication of the results of such studies. It is not a part of their function to determine, control, or influence the conduct of particular investigations or the conclusions reached." The immediate direction of the policies, program, and staff of the Institution is vested in the President, who is assisted by an advisory council, chosen from the professional staff of the Institution.

In publishing a study the Institution presents it as a competent treatment of a subject worthy of public consideration. The interpretations and conclusions in such publications are those of the author or authors and do not necessarily reflect the views of other members of the Brookings staff or of the administrative officers of the Institution.

Foreword

THIS EXPLORATORY study of the job of the federal executive and of the environment in which he works is the result of round table discussions held at the Brookings Institution in the early months of 1957. On the invitation of the Institution a group of distinguished federal executives and a few other persons met regularly for a series of evening meetings at which they considered (1) the nature of the executive's role and his job, (2) the differences in the functions of political and career executives, (3) the special characteristics of the environment in which the federal executive operates, (4) the problem of obtaining and developing effective federal executives. The members of the round table group are identified and the procedures followed are outlined in the introduction to the study.

The round table series was undertaken as a means of drawing upon the rich experience of those engaged in executive work of the federal government. It was thought that by means of these discussions some of the personal experience and judgments of these executives could be recorded so as to give others a better insight into the tasks and operating problems of career and political executives. This volume is a result of that effort. It gives the reader the essence of the discussions.

The round table meetings were under the able chairmanship of Professor Wallace S. Sayre of Columbia University. Professor Marver H. Bernstein of Princeton University served as executive secretary and developed the agenda for the meetings. To them and to the other participants the Institution is deeply indebted. Professor Bernstein has prepared the present volume from the recorded discussions and other pertinent and readily available material. The Brookings Institution is deeply indebted to him for the skill with which the materials have been brought together.

The Institution and the author wish to record their indebtedness to all the participants for reviewing the manuscript and making constructive suggestions. They are especially grateful for the assistance provided by John J. Corson, Paul T. David, Roger W. Jones, John W. Macy, Jr., and Wallace S. Sayre, who served as an Advisory Committee to review the manuscript in its final stages. The manuscript was completed for publication during Dr. David's tenure as Director of Governmental Studies at Brookings.

The round table and this publication were made possible by a grant from the McKinsey Foundation for Management Research, for which the Brookings Institution expresses its grateful appreciation.

The opinions and interpretations contained in this publication are those of the participants and the author and were reached wholly independent of the McKinsey Foundation, which is not to be understood as approving or disapproving the views expressed herein.

ROBERT D. CALKINS
President

June 1958

Contents

I

Introducing the Round Table

IN 1953 A PARTY that had been out of executive power
for two decades faced up to the task of directing the
federal government. Among its problems, the new administration found one to be unexpectedly vexing: How
could it recruit for scores of executive positions in a way
that would reconcile political requirements with the need
for competency in managing the government? Where could
qualified administrators be found? How could they be
attracted to government jobs? How could they be oriented
quickly and effectively to their new surroundings and
new responsibilities? Throughout early 1953 the problem
aroused considerable public interest and it was evident
that the staffing of key federal positions, both political and
career, required fresh study. Later that year the Task Force
on Personnel and Civil Service of the second Hoover Commission was organized to investigate this problem among
others.

The Task Force Report in 1955, and the ensuing controversy inside and outside the government, have made it
clear not only that the shortage of qualified federal executives is still a key issue, but also that the executive's job in
government is itself a proper subject of inquiry. Indeed,
there is very little published information on what federal
executives really do.

1

Government reports, professional periodicals and published studies in public administration, psychology, and sociology collectively tell little about the work of the federal executive, his relation to Congress and congressional committees, and his working relationships with other executives. The available publications tend to stress the need to improve personnel and personnel practices in the federal government but reveal little about the triumphs and failures, and the satisfactions and frustrations of government executives.

Despite the time and effort that the Eisenhower administration has devoted to the recruitment and retention of qualified executives, little orientation has been provided to help new executives understand their unfamiliar surroundings or the distinctive characteristics of their new jobs. Hundreds of able men with little previous experience in governmental affairs have had to serve in top posts without benefit of any systematic introduction to public life. They have had no adequate way of learning about the political setting of their jobs, the tasks and roles that characterize executive positions, and the pitfalls they might encounter.

The study of government affairs has also been handicapped by the shortage of books and other materials that help to explain the jobs of federal executives. Teachers of government have had few accounts that would give their students an understanding of this aspect of modern government, and few tests for the validity of generalizations that are frequently made about the management of federal programs and activities.

In recognition of this need for a better understanding of the work of federal executives, the Brookings Institution in 1957 assembled a group of distinguished political and career executives in the federal government for a discussion of this subject. Organized as the Round Table on the Federal Executive, the group of 24 members discussed the environment that surrounds the federal executive, influences his job, and provides and limits his opportunities.[1]

The Round Table met eight times, usually at bi-weekly intervals, in the period from February through April 1957. A final session was held in April 1958 to review the earlier discussions. The members usually arrived at the Brookings Institution about 6:15 p.m., dined together, and began discussions about 7:45 p.m. The sessions closed at 10 p.m. For each session the executive secretary prepared an agenda of discussion questions and a summary of the preceding discussion. Both papers were distributed to the members several days before the session. A verbatim transcript of the discussions served as the basis of the present volume. The discussions were confidential, and it was agreed that comments and statements would not be attributed to individuals or published without their consent. That is why quotations from the transcript are made throughout this volume without attribution of the statement to the speaker and without footnote reference to the transcript. While the prepared agenda helped to focus discussion and encourage members to think about the announced topics in advance of the sessions, members were not limited to discussing items specifically noted on the agenda nor did they feel constrained to avoid other subjects that interested them.

The Round Table provided an opportunity for a group of federal executives of demonstrated insight and experience to talk frankly and spontaneously about their part in

[1] For a list of Round Table members, see pp. 8-9.

running federal agencies. As one member stated at the final session:

> As far as I am aware, this effort has not been attempted before. These discussions suggest that much more can be done to make effective use of the accumulated experience of executives who have been through the mill, especially in preparing political executives coming in fresh from other fields.

A former federal executive noted how rare it is to get at first hand the frank remarks of experienced political and career executives about their work:

> What we have here is a product of their considered thinking over a period of several months. A group of men representing a wide variety of experience and background have spent a great deal of time together talking over problems with each other. I hope all of us realize how hard it is to come by such a product. In the past, most of the information we have had about the sort of questions discussed here has been the result of interviews conducted by a student or researcher with executives, one by one. This type of inquiry is in some respects much less revealing than a group discussion in which the remarks of one person are qualified, enriched, and occasionally contradicted by people with equally valuable but different experience.

Some comments about the Round Table may help to introduce this report of its discussions. First of all, as a technique, the Round Table appears to be a useful and productive method of inquiry appropriate to some aspects of public affairs. Organized group discussion may be viewed as a method of discovering information as well as a way of transmitting information. It may provide a way of approaching some problems that are not amenable to traditional research methods. A student of public administration remarked: "Our conversations indicate a method of discovery of information, knowledge, and insight; and perhaps they transmit a greater sense of reality than most of the literature of public administration with which I am acquainted."

Secondly, the Round Table discussions reveal a natural and inevitable emphasis on problems and difficulties rather than achievements. One member put it this way:

> We have been dealing not with the triumphs of federal executives but with their difficulties and, sometimes, their failures. We had to examine the problems. In session after session, we looked for difficulties and obstacles that remain to be overcome. Naturally, in the finished product, the obstacles loom larger than the rewards.

The conversational method and the frankness of the discussion helped to focus attention on matters that were troubling the members. The fact that all of them greatly valued their federal job experience and derived great satisfaction from it was more or less taken for granted throughout the discussions until the very end. As one member said half facetiously after reading this report in manuscript:

> Perhaps the published account might carry the following preface: "The accompanying book is distributed to assist new federal executives to understand their jobs and the environment in which they work. Notwithstanding the various complaints voiced herein, all of the participants nevertheless were happy to remain in the federal service."

As the emphasis on problems suggests, the Round Table did not attempt to provide a "balanced" view of the political setting of the federal executive or the nature of his job.

Similarly in discussing particular aspects of the executive's job—for example, his relationships with Congress and congressional committees and their staffs—the members tried to interpret their own experience in modern government, not to present a full, rounded analysis based on a careful assessment of all the data available.

Thirdly, the Round Table has emphasized the limits of traditional generalizations about American politics and especially about the administration of governmental programs.

> What we have here is the expression of highly varied experience about the way in which the federal government operates. These discussions provide some insights into the work of government which we do not find in the conventional literature based on sources that provide a more simplified and much less accurate picture of the way in which the administrative process moves along. Again and again we encounter indications of how limited are most of the generalizations on which we have been working. Almost every generalization we offered in discussion resulted in a chorus around the table that this generalization would have to be qualified, that reality was more complex, or that reality was different from the simplified generalization.

In the fourth place, the Round Table had clearly in mind the kinds of problems encountered by a business-oriented administration. Because the men who joined the Eisenhower administration as executives came primarily from business, much of the discussion is concerned with the attitudes and expectations of businessmen who come to Washington. Furthermore, it tends to emphasize the lack of preparation of many businessmen for government work. On the other hand, it is important to remember that individuals from other backgrounds also have things to learn if they are to function effectively in the political setting of Washington. Certainly this is true of farmers, labor leaders, state and local politicians, and not least, university professors. However, since the business community remains in all likelihood the most important single source of executive talent available to government, frequent contrasts between the environments of business and government and between business and government executives seem justified.

It was the hope of the Brookings Institution that the Round Table might make a contribution to students and scholars of American politics, to civil servants who develop careers in the public service, and especially, as a member of the Round Table stated, "to those who take executive posts in Washington and face a rugged experience in adapting to the governmental environment." As the Round Table reviewed its activities, it felt that its contribution might lie mainly in four areas: the wide-ranging diversity in the jobs of federal executives; the relationship of executives to Congress; the relationships of political and career executives; and significant differences between executive jobs in government and outside.

Members of the Round Table are listed on the following pages.

Round Table Participants[2]

JAMES V. BENNETT, Director, Bureau of Prisons, Department of Justice

MARVER H. BERNSTEIN, Associate Professor of Politics, Princeton University, Executive Secretary of the Round Table

ROBERT D. CALKINS, President, The Brookings Institution

JOHN J. CORSON, partner, McKinsey and Company, Management Consultants

PAUL. T. DAVID, Director of Governmental Studies, The Brookings Institution

O. GORDON DELK, Deputy Commissioner of Internal Revenue, Department of the Treasury

JOHN H. DILLON, Administrative Assistant to the Secretary of the Navy, Department of Defense (participated in two of the eight sessions)

HENRY A. DuFLON, Director, McKinsey Foundation for Management Research, Inc.

ROWLAND EGGER, Chairman, Department of Political Science, University of Virginia

DR. ROBERT H. FELIX, Director, National Institute of Mental Health, United States Public Health Service, Department of Health, Education, and Welfare

HENRY H. FOWLER, senior member, Fowler, Leva, Hawes, and Symington

[2] Participants are identified by the positions they held at the time of the conferences.

ROGER W. JONES, Assistant Director for Legislative Reference, Bureau of the Budget

EUGENE J. LYONS, Assistant Postmaster General and head of the Bureau of Personnel, Post Office Department

JOHN W. MACY, JR., Executive Director, United States Civil Service Commission

RICHARD E. MCARDLE, Chief, Forest Service, Department of Agriculture

WILFRED J. MCNEIL, Assistant Secretary of Defense and Comptroller, Department of Defense

RUFUS E. MILES, JR., Director of Administration, Department of Health, Education, and Welfare

GEORGE T. MOORE, Assistant Secretary of Commerce for Administration, Department of Commerce

WILLIAM W. PARSONS, Administrative Assistant Secretary, Department of the Treasury

JOHN A. PERKINS, Under Secretary, Department of Health, Education, and Welfare

WALLACE S. SAYRE, Professor of Public Administration, Department of Public Law and Government, Columbia University, Chairman of the Round Table

MARCELLUS C. SHEILD, former head of staff, Committee on Appropriations, United States House of Representatives

JAMES R. WIGGINS, Executive Editor, *Washington Post and Times Herald*

FELIX E. WORMSER, Assistant Secretary for Mineral Resources, Department of the Interior

II

The Job of the Political Executive

THE TERM "political executive," which has become important in the vocabulary of official Washington during the 1950's, was defined by the Round Table on the Federal Executive as any appointee, outside the civil service, who has policy-making duties.[1] The Round Table was concerned primarily with presidential appointees at the level of under secretary and assistant secretary; it confined itself mainly to executives in Washington and dealt only peripherally with executives in field offices. However, the category of federal political executives also includes heads of agencies, bureau chiefs appointed outside the civil service, and certain subordinate political appointees.

There are about 1,100 political executive positions in the federal government. About 100 of these positions have been created since 1954 when the Task Force on Personnel

[1] The second Hoover Commission preferred to use the term "non-career" rather than "political" in classifying political appointments outside the civil service. It apparently feared that "political" had an invidious connotation and should be avoided. It stated: "It is generally understood that the Nation requires non-career executives who serve at the pleasure of the President and his immediate department and agency heads and who represent the political party in power and the measures to which it is committed." U.S. Commission on Organization of the Executive Branch of the Government, *Personnel and Civil Service*, A Report to the Congress (1955) p. 25.

and Civil Service of the second Hoover Commission estimated the number as follows:[2]

Heads of agencies and their deputies	230
Assistant agency heads	125
General managers of boards and commissions	10
Non-civil service bureau chiefs	250[3]
Subordinate executives	390
Heads of substantive staff offices 40	
Heads of departmental information offices 50	
Political aides and assistants 300	

Total 1,005

WHAT POLITICAL EXECUTIVES DO

The second Hoover Commission tended to view the job of the political executive as a composite of tasks. The major ones include taking command of departments and agencies, developing policies and programs, defending these before Congress, the public, and presidential staff arms such as the Bureau of the Budget, making political speeches, and participating in political activities to promote his party's position.[4] The Commission's Task Force on Personnel emphasized the functions of the political executive in providing political leadership:

In the National Government, it is the function of political executives to represent within the administration the

[2] U.S. Commission on Organization of the Executive Branch of the Government, *Task Force Report on Personnel and Civil Service* (1955), pp. 16, 22, 39.

[3] The Task Force found that 190 of 266 bureau chiefs in 45 major agencies were exempt from civil service. If the same proportion of the bureau chiefs in all agencies (350) are appointed outside the civil service, their number would be 250.

[4] *Personnel and Civil Service,* A Report to the Congress, p. 27.

policy purposes of the President, to bring the general public's point of view to bear upon administrative decisions, to provide leadership in developing national policy, to exercise statutory powers vested in them as public officials, and to act for the Chief Executive in seeing that all of the laws are faithfully executed; in short, to take the responsibility for governing.[5]

In November 1946, Donald C. Stone contributed to the Princeton University Bicentennial Conference on University Education and the Public Service an analysis of the setting in which the federal administrator works. Stone included in his category of "top managers" the heads of departments and agencies, their principal operating and staff assistants, and similar officials in the bureaus and other major subdivisions within agencies. These various executives, comprising presumably both political and nonpolitical appointees, were defined functionally in the following terms:

Their energies are devoted, broadly speaking, to defining the objectives of their agencies, planning the program, developing an organization properly staffed to carry out the program, scheduling and budgeting the program, developing the necessary interrelationships, channels of communication, work habits, and doctrine for the organization to move forward as a harmonious team, establishing devices for control and coordination, exercising oversight and guiding the operations of the establishment, and maintaining and reacting to many external relationships.[6]

It is clear from the context of Stone's description that no single executive performs all or most of these functions.

---

[5] *Task Force Report on Personnel and Civil Service,* p. 1.

[6] Donald C. Stone, "The Top Manager and His Environment," Joseph E. McLean, ed., *The Public Service and University Education* (1949), p. 51.

Rather, the statement covers a range of tasks encompassing the entire sequence of command and direction within an organization. With this qualification in mind, the Round Table considered the validity of Stone's job description. A career executive commented:

My impression is that his definition indicates what somebody thought a political executive ought to do rather than what he usually does. For example, the first item is the defining of objectives. By and large, the objectives of agencies are spelled out in law and practice prior to the appointment of executives, who have to spend a good deal of their time finding out what these objectives are. Moreover, as quickly as political executives come into office, they have to resist pressures that would make them prisoners of their agencies. They have to meet so many demands, make so many contacts, process so much paper, and attend so many meetings all at once that they have little time for such matters as defining objectives. There is an inexorable Gresham's Law of public administration: Day-to-day problems tend to drive out long-range planning. Only the most astute executive is able to organize his time to fend off outside pressures and internal office routine sufficiently to leave adequate time to deal with longer range items.

Three other executives commented as follows:

This sounds like a definition of the job of an executive during World War II or the Korean War who faced the task of creating a new program and a new staff to administer it. The typical political executive comes into an established federal agency from private life. This statement is more applicable to an executive who did not have any predecessors.

The definition seems to apply primarily to career executives in staff positions. The last of the eight functions listed in the definition—maintaining and reacting to external relationships—seems to be an afterthought, although it is the one element of the definition that presumably identifies the political executive clearly and distinguishes him from the corporation executive. All the other elements are focussed primarily inward. This is not a description of an executive who is responsible for some government activity. It fits better the political program or staff type of person who utilizes his time to develop a program, evaluate performance, set objectives, and so forth. The line operator wouldn't begin to have the time to do all the things in this definition.

In order to make this definition applicable to the political executive, it would have to include the task of harmonizing the programs of his agency with the political point of view and the aspirations of his party. The political executive has the task of assuring that his subordinates are loyally following that program. Instead of defining the objectives of his agency, he must make certain that the agency conforms to the policy of the administration.

There was general agreement that in any agency a number of people perform these functions, but the daily job of a single executive does not encompass all of them. A political executive has broad responsibility for all eight functions, but he is apt to devote a major part of his time to external relations and to rely in varying degrees on subordinates to perform the other functions. The definition indicates the range of his responsibility, but gives a misleading picture of the way he spends his time.

Once again, generalizations are hazardous. Political appointees come from a variety of occupational and professional backgrounds. They bring to the task of political leadership differing views toward government and their roles within the government. Executives drawn from corporate management, investment firms, law offices, universities, federal civil service, metropolitan government, and public service in predominantly rural states may have little in common beyond their temporary willingness to serve their government.

It is useful to keep in mind an obvious characteristic of the work of executives, both in business and government. Management can rarely achieve its aims by command alone. Men do not spring into action when buttons are pressed and orders go down the line. Authority is not automatically enforced. The task of management, both public and private, is to provide the kind of leadership that produces spontaneous and cooperative effort rather than to impose authoritative decisions. What the executive "achieves is largely the product of his influence rather than his command. Therefore, in long range terms, the job of an executive is to create an environment conducive to concerted effort in pursuit of the organization's objectives."[7]

In a civil service system that makes employees relatively secure and in an unstable environment that makes political executives relatively insecure, the obstacles confronting the executive seeking to maximize his influence on his organization are formidable and frustrating. They can be overcome only by executives who understand the governmental environment and who combine a capacity for popular leadership with a capacity for management of large-scale, complex enterprises.

Examples of How They Spend Their Time.   Because of differences in departmental organization and functions and

[7] Donald C. Stone, "Notes on the Governmental Executive: His Role and His Methods," *New Horizons in Public Administration* (1945), p. 48.

variations in personality and competence among political executives, it was not possible for the Round Table to draft a meaningful standard job description for federal political executives. But comments by various participants do suggest the range of the executive's activities. Even within the level of assistant secretary in a major department, jobs vary significantly.

Assistant Secretary A heads one of five bureaus in a large cabinet department. He, as well as the other four assistant secretaries, had considerable experience in private business relevant to his governmental assignment. Mr. A, who deals principally with personnel management, was active in general management and personnel administration in business. The enormous size of the working force of the department requires the assistant secretaries to devote a substantial percentage of their time to managerial activities. Mr. A described how he spent his time:

> My day depends pretty heavily on whether Congress is in session. Assuming that Congress is in session, I spend about one third of my time in direct contact with members of Congress, committee staffs, and other governmental agencies. If I add the time I spend with other persons not engaged in departmental activities, the proportion of time spent with outsiders would probably rise at least to 40 per cent and perhaps as much as 50 per cent. The rest of my time is split between direct technical management of the bureau I head, and over-all departmental problems which involve meetings and conferences with the Secretary and the other assistant secretaries.
>
> My normal working day is roughly nine hours. The time for thinking and planning is usually the first hour of the morning, because I happen to get to the office before anyone else does. I can also do some serious reflection and

thinking between 5:15 and 6:15 in the afternoon after the phones stop ringing constantly, but that hour is not included in the nine hours.

I don't mean to leave the impression that most of my days can be divided into these time spans. If the department has an important bill up for consideration on the Hill, I may spend almost all of my time for several weeks on legislative matters, but taking the year as a whole, that is roughly how it goes.

I try to save time by delegating broad responsibilities to my division heads. Some of these tasks involve continuing relations with industrial groups on semi-technical matters. The daily contacts with these organized groups are handled mostly by the division heads. Most of the group contacts can be delegated downward in the organization.

Assistant Secretary B supervises a cluster of bureaus and offices in a department that employs about 50,000 persons. Before becoming a political executive, he served as a senior executive in a large corporation and had developed a consulting service in his technical field. He described his work as follows:

My work day is pretty long. I get to the office about 8:30 and leave about 6:00 or 6:30, and I take work home with me almost every evening. The distribution of my time depends upon Congress. If the department is subject to legislative pressure, I have to give that business top priority. During the last investigation that concerned me, I spent about 90 per cent of my time testifying before committees or else getting ready for the next day's appearance.

It is very difficult to prevent your work from becoming a succession of telephone calls, meetings, and documents. I try to screen my contacts as much as possible. Perhaps the best time I have for thinking is when I am shaving.

About 20 per cent of my time is spent talking with the heads of the bureaus under my supervision or reading their reports. That may be less time than other executives devote to this work, but I depend as much as I can on monthly and other reports to keep me informed about our activities. I often take these reports home with me in the evening when I can look at them leisurely.

I have always felt that an executive must have face-to-face contacts, and I encourage them. I try to screen them to avoid waste of time. A great volume of correspondence comes across my desk, but a lot of it is fortunately answered before it reaches me. I scrutinize it, see how many people have cleared it, and sign it. I do not have a great deal of personal dictation, but I try to write my own speeches in order to reflect my own ideas and personality. This takes an extraordinary amount of time, but it is rewarding. I have constant calls from senators and congressmen; I try to accommodate them on the phone. If necessary I go to chat with them directly. All in all, these congressional contacts on individual matters probably take no more than 5 per cent of my time.

At least one third of my day is devoted to interdepartmental conferences and committee meetings on defense mobilization affairs, foreign economic policy, public policy toward certain domestic industries, and so forth. These meetings usually lead to important policy decisions; consequently, preparation for them requires a lot of time. I have such a meeting practically every day.

I try to delegate to the bureaus almost all contacts with industry, labor, and other nongovernmental groups. I feel it is important for the bureaus to have those contacts. I get my industry contacts when I attend a business convention, make a speech, and chat informally away from the office. Some of the bureaus I supervise are strictly scientific in their work; they have few industrial contacts that require my attention. But other bureaus active in economic affairs must maintain their industrial contacts. We have depended in this general area rather heavily upon industry advisory committees, and they have been very helpful to us. On the whole, delegation of nongovernmental contacts to the bureaus has worked well.

Factors Influencing Executive Behavior. The distribution of a political executive's time depends partly upon his disposition to dig deeply into some matters and to stay removed from others. As a career bureau chief remarked, an assistant secretary can usually make some choices about the depth of his direct participation in particular decisions:

> I have had some political executives as bosses who did not want to get into certain fields, and left those decisions to me. And I have had some who wanted to make all decisions. The job of the bureau chief is to find out where certain types of decisions are going to be made.

Organization factors also influence the job of the assistant secretary. In a department headed by a secretary, an under secretary, and one assistant secretary, the bureau chief usually exercises more discretion in making policy decisions. In departments with an under secretary and a corps of assistant secretaries, these officials are likely to maintain closer control over bureau policy. The relationship of an assistant secretary to his bureau chief depends on how well-informed the former is about the work of the bureaus, the degree of compatibility between the two levels of direction, and the competence and experience of the assistant secretary. To some extent an assistant secretary serves as an appellate body, to whom outsiders may go if their wants are not satisfied by the bureau chief. If the assistant secretary frequently overrules his bureau chiefs in their dealings with outside groups, those groups will be tempted to come directly to the assistant secretary who will then become more involved in administrative details and nongovernmental contacts.

The budget process also takes considerable time. Emphasis upon budgeting varies greatly from agency to agency, but most political executives are exposed to a perpetual cycle of estimates, Budget Bureau clearances, appropriations hearings, allotments and allocation of appropriated funds, supplemental estimates, and deficiency estimates. An assistant secretary commented: "I was on the Hill this morning testifying on my estimates. I will be back tomorrow morning also. You no sooner finish with one appropriation matter than a new one comes."

As in other matters, however, the political executive may or may not, as he chooses, become involved in the details of the budget process. An assistant bureau chief noted:

> Quite often a lawyer without previous executive experience becomes an assistant secretary. He tends to bury himself in the details of budget estimates, just as if he were preparing a case for trial. When he realizes that he is swamped with work he cannot handle, he usually seeks assistance. On the other hand, an assistant secretary with previous executive experience will probably concentrate more on establishing program objectives and broad cost determinations and then rely on the bureau chiefs for detailed estimates. As long as the bureau officers are able to support the secretary's program decisions, the assistant secretary does not get substantially involved in the budget process. But if something goes wrong, he will step in quickly.

The budget process raises many interesting and relevant questions. For example, does it help an agency to have its estimate presented to Congress by a political executive who belongs to the same party as the chairman of the appropriations subcommittee? Or is it better to have the estimate presented by the individual who is thoroughly familiar with its details? One participant who has observed the appropriations process in Congress closely for many years replied:

> Generally speaking, in my experience the fellow who has fared best in presenting budget estimates to Congress is the one who knows what he is talking about and makes an impression on the committee as a good administrator. If such a fellow is utterly frank, lays his cards on the table, and impresses the committee with his competence and knowledge, he gets along well except in those cases where there is some special political aspect. It is tragic to see the political head of a department or bureau, in testimony before a committee, forced to turn to his career staff to answer simple questions about the operations of his agency. If a political executive doesn't know much about his agency, the committee will soon find it out. It is much better for that political executive to send somebody from his office who does know the details of operation to represent the bureau or department.

Executives who are deeply involved in negotiations with Congress, interdepartmental conferences, cabinet committees, interest groups, and internal managerial problems are not likely to have much time for leisurely thinking and analysis. Instead they have to rely on other people to help them do their thinking. The staff cannot do it all, but it can supply the background and framework. Frenzied activity to meet the deadlines of a congressional committee or to frustrate the appropriation-cutting objectives of the Bureau of the Budget may seem to make thoughtful consideration of problems and issues by political executives almost impossible. Nevertheless, their jobs make heavy demands on them for clarity of thought, analytical judgment and apt expression. A close observer stated:

> Political executives in recent administrations have not usually been as expert in their subject matter fields as their technical staffs. But the fact remains that they were able, within their own departments, in interdepartmental committees, in the White House, and before committees on the Hill to think through some difficult problems. They have been able to come out with the kind of answer that is normally required in American politics: a backing away from the original position into a modified program that somehow blends with the desires of competing interests and the wishes of Congress.

However a political executive spends his time, much of his work is designed to protect his agency and the integrity of its programs. A career executive characterized this process as "defending the empire":

> The field of federal activities today is finely fragmented across a very broad spectrum. There is scarcely a political executive in town whose jurisdiction does not overlap that of some other agency and some other executive. If he is going to do the job that the President and his secretary expect of him, he will have to develop a carefully calculated and highly polished belligerency in defense of his agency. In time this becomes almost a reflex action, and at that point it may lead to a dangerous overconfidence or aggressiveness. But the fact remains that the political environment is highly competitive as well as actually or potentially unstable. Active rather than passive defense is crucial to survival.

The political executive's social life presents some special problems and hazards in Washington. Opportunities for socializing at lunches, dinners, cocktail parties, and receptions are superabundant. For some executives, social activity within and outside of office hours represents a substantial part of their lives and those of their wives. The apparent "demands" of the social season in Washington may even make a significant dent in their personal incomes. However, success on the job need not depend on after-hours activities. Much depends on the attitude and fortitude of the individual executive and his wife. Some executives perform their jobs successfully although they are rarely seen at social affairs. The military departments have had a number of executives whose success was not dependent on their extra-curricular activities. As Secretary of War, Henry Stimson was quite austere. As Assistant Secretary of War for Air and Under Secretary of State, Robert Lovett attended few social functions. Secretary of the Navy Forrestal, as a Defense Department official stated, "did pretty much as he pleased." As Secretary of State, George C. Marshall accepted few invitations.

Dealing with Technical Matters.   One of the most difficult recurrent problems facing the political executive is the extent to which he should deal with technical matters. There is general agreement that executives ought not to become deeply involved in them, but there is no accepted way of distinguishing policy making from technical work. The depth of policy tends to vary from agency to agency. In some agencies, the major tasks of the staff are related to the framing of decisions. In a few agencies, the overriding characteristic is management of routine, non-discretionary activities. Occasionally some matters may appear deceptively technical. The Internal Revenue Service, for example, may have to decide whether a particular group or individual comes within the meaning of the term "church" in order to determine tax liability, or whether a particular organization qualifies as a "charitable organization," thereby making contributions to it tax-exempt. The tax laws are general and offer administrators little guidance. While these matters appear to be technical details, they are likely to have marked political implications. If so, political executives may have to review the proposals or decisions of the career staff.

The tendency of technical staffs to resist executive control seems to be common to both government and business. A former federal executive said: "I used to think that only insurance actuaries said: 'Don't ask me why. Just take my word for it.' During the past few years I have spent time with oil companies. There the geologists behave the same way. The geologist says: 'Don't ask me why. Just drill where I say because I say so.'"

The tendency to dip into technical matters depends somewhat on previous technical and executive experience. An experienced executive is likely to be more aware of the importance of "operating on his proper level," that is, dealing with major matters of program, policy, and political involvement and avoiding technical work as much as possible. Moreover, an executive with a particular technical background may have an important advantage. One executive stated: "When a man comes into government in an executive post in a field in which he has some familiarity, he can ask the technicians questions earlier. The good executive starts out asking questions and is still asking questions."

If some executives have technical backgrounds, technicians are not necessarily devoid of political skills and instincts:

The technician's political instinct may be only to protect a vested interest in the know-how of doing something. Sometimes it may be an effort to please by anticipating the information that an executive wants to have. And sometimes it may lead to action designed to sabotage the political purposes of the political executive. I was present once when a Secretary of Agriculture asked an economist for some statistics on burley tobacco. The economist stopped at the door and asked: "What do you want to prove, Mr. Secretary?" Every executive has a risky relationship with his technical staff, some of whom really resist his decisions and some of whom are so anxious to conform to it that they distort their technical competence. The fellow who becomes an executive in a department in which he has had a lot of technical experience is very fortunate, but the average federal executive doesn't have the advantage of being as well equipped technically as his subordinates. He has to define as best he can the point at which he feels safe in asking questions, using his own judgment, or imposing a decision about which the technicians have misgivings. This is one of the greatest challenges facing an executive.

The capacity of an executive to question and control his technical staff is most severely tested in the military departments. American experience suggests that the survival risks are high when a political executive questions the military officer-technicians in the Department of Defense.

One safeguard available to the political executive is to

put qualified technicians on his own staff to review the staff work of the bureau technicians. Through the competition of the two technical staffs, the executive can be relatively assured of obtaining the benefit of completed staff work before decisions are made.

BUSINESS AND POLITICAL JOBS COMPARED

In many respects, the job of the executive in business is similar to the job of the political executive in the federal government. Both must lay out work plans for future activities, maintain a going establishment, secure adequate funds and staffing, and evaluate performance. Like his political counterpart, the business executive confers with subordinates and associates, attends conferences and meetings, justifies and defends his program before a board of directors, signs correspondence, concerns himself with personnel problems, and undertakes a variety of social activities to maximize his influence in his organization or industry. Yet the nature of the job of the political executive in Washington, the operating problems, and the relevant personal factors appear to be fundamentally different in many strategic particulars from executive jobs in private employment and in other governments.

The Nature of the Job.   Undoubtedly, differences between executive jobs in business and government are in part differences in scale. In terms of magnitude of operations—numbers of employees, levels of expenditures, range of activities, and impact on the public—few business enterprises match the programs of the federal government. Most political executives who have been trained in private business have never before managed affairs on so massive a scale. Many of them have had experience in relatively small businesses where the scope of their activity was narrowly confined. Few executives acquire in business the quality that enables them to handle relationships in large-scale operations in their larger and broader terms. This quality has been defined as "a capacity to see public policy in terms of thousands of different actions and to relate these actions to each other in terms of public and governmental interest. . . . It must embody the logic of events and sentiments, and not merely the logic of statistics."[8] The adjustment that most executives from business must make in their government jobs is necessitated by quantitative and qualitative differences in the nature of the executive's job in business and government.

Political executives lead much less sheltered lives than their business counterparts. Lack of privacy in the political environment calls for a different approach to the job. "The political executive must weigh very carefully the impression that he makes on the public. He must consider how his operations will be regarded by the general public and a lot of specialized publics, like interest groups and key congressional figures." Unlike the business executive, the political executive must anticipate vilification and a possible withholding of public prestige and trust.

The public nature of the executive's job in government has no precise parallel in business. Accountability of business executives to corporate boards of directors, stockholders, and consumers is highly restricted compared to the constant exposure of political executives to "the public." As Struve Hensel, formerly assistant secretary of the Navy remarked:

[8] Paul Appleby, *Big Democracy* (1945), p. 43.

The sky . . . is the limit with respect to the public and its servants. Public accountability of the governmental administrator is a night and day affair. He is bombarded with letters of criticism and demand. His administration is investigated publicly and privately. The people's representatives in Congress seem tireless in the pursuit of the administrator. It is impossible to please all of the congressmen at any time. In addition, there are the self-appointed investigators, the commentators, columnists, and private scandal seekers. Each one has a special angle and the newspapers seem to prefer stories of mistake and disagreement. Worst of all, the public is most fickle and changeable. Administrative programs and procedures which ignore the possible desires of the people or, to use more dignified language, the political implications, cannot hope to succeed, irrespective of soundness in logic or economics.[9]

The executive's job in government seems to require both a sensitivity to public desires and a capacity to absorb considerable abuse. Unless the political executive becomes accustomed to the irritations as well as the necessity of public scrutiny and cultivates an ability to anticipate popular reaction and major shifts in political movements and national sentiments, his effectiveness on the job may be sharply limited and his survival potential minimal.

One characteristic of the job of the political executive that perplexes the recent recruit from business is the willingness of the executive branch to tolerate and even encourage open disputes between agencies on unresolved issues. In business, generally speaking, controversies over internal business policy are not debated in public except in connection with stockholder revolts against incumbent

[9] H. Struve Hensel, "Problems of Structure and Personnel," Joseph E. McLean, ed., *op. cit.*, p. 83.

corporate management. To the business executive, an open conflict between two or more agencies on an important issue suggests a breakdown in teamwork and a failure of management. To the experienced political executives, such conflict may be inconvenient and troublesome but perhaps the best or only way of identifying the public interest in a controversial area of public policy.

An incident recalled by an assistant secretary illustrates the point.

> During my first few months on the job, I was asked to deal with a proposed international agreement for the stabilization of the price of tin. My staff told me that this agreement had been seven years in the making and that the State Department was anxious to have it approved. My investigation disclosed that the Secretary of the Treasury, the Secretary of Commerce, and others were opposed to the agreement. I proceeded to oppose it as not in line with the President's program. One day I was called to the Commerce Department to attend a meeting of an industry advisory committee to discuss the tin agreement. I had opposed the State Department on the approval of the agreement, but I had done so within the executive branch. Now I was asked to debate the agreement with an assistant secretary of State in public before the industry committee. He made an impassioned plea to approve the tin agreement on political grounds, while I opposed it and called attention to its economic implications.

A few years later, this assistant secretary testified before the House Armed Services Committee on the problem of oil shale reserves. The Navy wanted to operate a government oil shale plant which the Interior Department wanted to shut down and rely instead on private industry. He remarked: "The spectacle of two departments arguing publicly before a congressional committee was not a very edifying example of teamwork in the executive branch."

A career executive with much governmental experience stated the case for open disputes among political executives:

> Public debate by executives on unresolved issues assumes a calculated risk of damaging the discipline within the executive branch. Such open controversy is strong medicine that must be taken in small doses. These disputes are very difficult for policy making officers to handle, but almost too easy at times for the career staff, which can become very blasé about the lack of integration in the government.

The political executive spends far more time than the business executive does in justifying his program and operations. One close observer has noted:

> Many officials complain that they must spend so much time in preparing for appearing at Congressional hearings and in presenting their programs before the Bureau of the Budget and other bodies that it often leaves little time for directing the operations of their agencies. Also, the necessity for checking proposed actions and for keeping complete records of their activities in case they must defend themselves absorbs a great deal of time which otherwise might be devoted to more constructive effort. All in all, it is small wonder that most government officials are found at their desks long after closing time or carry home a brief case of papers which "one of those days" prevented them from reviewing.[10]

Finally, the political executive's job is plainly a temporary assignment, while that of the business executive

---

[10] Stone, "The Top Manager and His Environment," Joseph E. McLean, ed., *op. cit.*, p. 56.

approximates a permanent one. In business, at least, employees must assume that their superiors are likely to be around for a long time and behave accordingly. In government, his expendability may induce in the executive an uneasy feeling that some of the career staff is merely marking time until he is replaced or, in extreme cases, is actively undermining his position.

Problems of Operation. Late in 1952, the Eisenhower cabinet-to-be attended many conferences with executives whose positions they were to assume shortly. A career executive who was privileged to attend many of these conferences said:

> Almost all of the new executives about to take over leading assignments in the cabinet expressed the very same thought. They had attended meetings and enlarged their governmental contacts over a period of several weeks. One thing in particular impressed them about government. They said, "In a business enterprise, the executive is always told in advance exactly what the aims and purposes are of the organization he is joining, and he is sold on those aims from the beginning. But in government, we have to find out for ourselves what the aims of our departments are and what our role is supposed to be as secretary." They were quite surprised and even shocked to realize how extensive their responsibilities would be and how much they were expected to know about a wide range of matters that somehow concerned their departments.

Uncertainty and lack of precision in defining objectives are especially troublesome in a change of administration that brings a party to power after a long period of minority status. The aims of administrations organized by the opposing party are suspect, while the new administration has not yet formulated its operating philosophy with sufficient clarity for application to the programs of various agencies. Objectives defined in enabling statutes, as new executives soon discover, leave considerable room for discretion in interpreting legislative intent. The major consequence of this situation is that the political executive often does not have available a ready-made, tested, acceptable statement of purpose or mission.

Business executives usually have more manageable jobs than political executives partly because the outer limits of their responsibility do not normally extend beyond the firm they help to direct. In Washington, however, a political executive is a part of the executive branch whose general purposes he is expected to advance. Getting things done requires activity that carries the executive into the nooks and crannies of the Executive Office of the President, several sets of legislative committees and their staffs, a host of interdepartmental committees, and a substantial number of individual bureaus and agencies. Lack of self-sufficiency in government programs usually forces the executive to concentrate half or more of his time on other than purely internal matters of administration. As one political executive stated: "One troubling aspect of the job of the political executive is that it usually takes much longer than it does in business to find out where to go to get things done. It is not easy to discover who should be consulted and whose toes must not be stepped on."

Perhaps the paramount distinction between executive jobs in government and business is the pervasive role of Congress in public administration.

No business executive ever had to deal with a board of overseers like Congress. Moreover, as a business executive,

I would never have dreamed of spending as much as one third of my time with my board of directors. In the corporation I served for many years, I spent perhaps a half day once a month with my board.

There are at least 436 reasons why the House of Representatives and 98 reasons why the Senate create difficulties. These difficulties are exaggerated by the executive's lack of political experience as well as his ineptness in dealing with Congress. As many successful political executives have proved, it is certainly possible to get along well with Congress without losing stature for the President. But one of the main requisites is the acquisition of special knowledge concerning legislative habits and procedures. A former political executive asserted:

It is axiomatic that the political executive must acquire as soon as he possibly can a fundamental understanding of how Congress operates and what the major legislative cycles are. Anyone not in government would probably fail to realize that you have to get the legislative ball started very early to get something considered. The sooner the executive recognizes that he has to get going in November in order to have a fighting chance to appear before legislative committees in May, the better off he will be.

An important difference between the executive task in government and that in business is the requirement in government of much more co-ordination.

If you have a high executive position in business, your orders are obeyed. You consult one or two people and you decide what to do. Coming from business into government, you are apt to be shocked to discover that almost all important questions of policy impinge on some other agency. You have to get the viewpoint of these agencies, and that takes time. Unless you move slowly and cautiously at the start, you are apt to bump your toes repeatedly. Perhaps the most important thing that the political executive from business has to learn is the necessity to adjust himself to the other man's point of view.

The authority of the political executive is circumscribed by the necessity for clearance and co-ordination in the executive branch. As one business analyst reported:

> Those who have experience in both business and politics observe that the political executive gains power in magnitude of operations, and loses in having to share with others the power of decision. Ability to share the power of decision with co-equals is the essential mark of the political executive.[11]

Many of the factors in the governmental environment—size, complexity of operations, built-in conflicts, and public accountability—have produced a growing emphasis on procedure and routine in public administration. Government has no monopoly on red tape and procedures that check performance. Any big organization must develop safeguards against fraud and deception, but integrity is demanded more completely in government than in any other large-scale undertaking. An executive with extensive experience in both business and government suggests that

> . . . no matter how well briefed on federal service peculiarities the private business executive may be, one of the first things he notices in public administration is this emphasis on procedure and routine. This emphasis is admittedly necessary and desirable provided it does not make method an end in itself. When it does, overorganized be-

[11] John McDonald, "The Businessman in Government," *Fortune*, Vol. 50 (July 1954), p. 156.

wilderment results. The newcomer to top management positions in the federal service frequently feels that the organization and methods set up with the laudable idea of keeping him from doing wrong actually result in making it
excessively difficult to do right.[12]

Personal Factors. In addition to differences in the nature of the job and in characteristic operating problems,
jobs of political and business executives differ in personal
involvement.

A former business executive now employed in government may be uncertain about the quality of his performance
because he has no tested standard for measuring performance. The profit standard familiar to him in business is not
transferable.

> In government the executive does not have the same
> measuring sticks to help him manage his affairs that the
> business executive has. He has nothing he can box and
> crate and put on the loading platform to be sold competi-
> tively. Lacking a familiar standard to appraise the real
> value of his management, he wonders how well he is man-
> aging his program.

In the turbulence of the Washington environment, an
executive may occasionally wonder whether he is really
needed. He may have given up an excellent job to serve
the administration in Washington and be part of the presidential team, only to discover later that his contacts with
the President are noticeably infrequent. In the hurly-burly
of interagency negotiations, he is uncertain about his
sources of support and the relationship of his activities to
the program of the President.

[12] Robert A. Lovett, "A Business Executive Looks at Government,"
Joseph E. McLean, ed., *op. cit.*, p. 71.

After a while, the fellow who comes to Washington is not so sure he is needed. He needs reassurance every two or three months because the apparent facts of his daily official life do not bear out the hope or contention that he is performing an essential service.

The insecurity of the political climate often makes executives more cautious. Since authority is rarely commensurate with legal responsibility, the executive must establish his own alliances and temporary coalitions within the executive branch. In this way, he may secure the clearances required to approve those policies that matter most to his program, but normally he may have to move carefully and exercise considerable skill in political negotiation.

The importance of negotiating skill is increased by the fact that while social and educational backgrounds of business executives tend toward homogeneity, those of political executives are marked by diversity. A political executive recruited from business explained:

> In a business company, most of the executives have the same sort of background. It is easy and comfortable for them to talk to each other and to accept one another. It is relatively easy to absorb a new executive who comes out of the same social circle and environment. But in my department the executives come in from various backgrounds and experience. Our group of under secretaries and assistant secretaries have little in common. We find that we do not even speak the same language, and we certainly don't talk the language of the career employee. When we became government executives, most of us were not familiar with the programs of our department or of other related government agencies. We didn't know what they did, and it took a long time for us to find out. For a business executive who tends to take it for granted that his executive associate or

key subordinate is the same sort of person he is, the job of the political executive is rather mystifying. It makes it hard to open up lines of communication with colleagues in government, and without these lines, it is almost impossible to be effective.

In contrast to the business executive, the political executive tends to work with a less homogeneous group of executives, administers programs that are generally larger in scope and public significance, lacks privacy in his unofficial as well as official life, and periodically undergoes trial by public debate. He must devote more time to a defense of his programs and policies even though his tenure on the job is relatively brief. Unlike the business executive, he directs activities that often lack a clearly defined purpose and that normally are matters of some concern to other political and career executives, congressional leaders and staffs, interest groups, and the general public. Except in rare cases, previous experience in private life has not prepared him adequately to deal effectively with Congress. On the other hand, the political executive has an opportunity that probably surpasses that provided by almost any executive post in private life for a stimulating experience, satisfaction in dealing with important matters on a large scale, and a self-respecting sense of service to his country.

III

The Job of the Career Executive

THE TERM "career executive" as used in this report designates a person serving under a civil service appointment and having high responsibility for the conduct of a governmental program. A career executive cannot be identified simply by the title of his position, because many career officials occupy positions similar to those held by political executives. The difference lies in the method of appointment and in the different orientation of the career man toward his duties.

At a minimum, the category of career executives includes about 400 to 500 civil service officials serving as deputy and assistant heads of agencies, executive assistants, bureau and staff office chiefs, and assistant bureau chiefs.[1] If the

[1] In its survey of top management officials from agency and department heads down to assistant bureau chiefs in forty of the more important and larger agencies in 1954, the Task Force on Personnel and Civil Service of the second Hoover Commission found that 29% or 374 out of 1,300 executives were appointed under the competitive civil service as follows:

No agency heads out of 133
12 deputy and assistant agency heads out of 101
46 executive assistants out of 233
143 bureau and staff office chiefs out of 434
173 assistant bureau chiefs out of 399

If the number of top managers is increased by 15 per cent to include executives in the remaining agencies, and the proportion of those appointed under civil service remains more or less the same, it can be

category is extended downward to include division chiefs, regional and district office directors, and most senior aides and assistants, it probably includes as many as 4,000 career officials.

It is not possible to designate as career executives all persons who occupy the so-called supergrade positions GS-16 to GS-18. Only about 6 out of 10 of these positions are subject to appointment under rules applicable to the competitive civil service. Of the 1,354 supergrade positions in 1957, 726 were civil service appointments and the remaining 628 positions were subject to appointment under Schedule A, B, or C or were at the discretion of the appointing official. In addition, many of these positions are not primarily executive in nature.

> A considerable number are lawyers, an even greater number are engineers and natural scientists, and others are economists, statisticians, and specialists in various fields of the social sciences who work primarily at their respective professional specialties. Most of these individuals act frequently as advisers to executives and most of them probably have limited executive responsibilities. Yet many of them are neither engaged in nor experienced in administration. . . .[2]

The Round Table discussions about the career executive were centered upon civil service appointees serving as professional administrators at the highest levels, particularly on bureau chiefs and their staff counterparts, administra-

concluded that there are about 400 to 500 civil service appointees in these positions. See U.S. Commission on Organization of the Executive Branch of the Government, *Task Force Report on Personnel and Civil Service* (1955), pp. 211-14.

[2] Paul T. David and Ross Pollock, *Executives for Government* (1957), p. 92.

tive assistant secretaries, and deputy heads of major bureaus and offices.

THE PROBLEM OF POLITICAL INVOLVEMENT

The most controversial aspect of the job of the career executive is his participation in policy decisions and his consequent involvement in the political process. The Round Table considered at length the proposal of the Hoover Commission Task Force on personnel to create a senior corps of politically neutral career executives.

The Proposal for a Senior Civil Service. The Task Force viewed the ideal career executive as a professional administrator experienced in the intricacies of public administration.

> It is the function of . . . career [executives] . . ., who must serve whatever responsible officials are in office, to provide a reservoir of knowledge, managerial competence based upon experience, and understanding of the peculiarities of Government administration. It is their job to keep the Government operating as effectively as possible at all times. They are essential to maintain the national administration as a going concern under all conditions. They can put political executives in touch with the long background behind most important issues, and help them to understand the probable consequences of alternative courses of action. They can also relieve political executives of the great burden of administrative detail involved in operating the vast governmental establishment.[3]

In the Task Force model, "political executives necessarily come and go in public office, and their expendability is an essential element in representative government." Their

[3] *Task Force Report on Personnel and Civil Service,* pp. 1-2.

task is to provide political leadership "in reconsidering old policies and methods and in seeking both better goals and better methods."[4] On the other hand, the career executive, according to the Task Force, must abjure political activity and remain neutral, although he is legally and morally committed to the public interest.

In touch with past experience, and familiar with the sometimes painful details of administration, he must emphasize matters of feasibility, practicability, and effectiveness. As a yes-man, he would be unfaithful to his duty, and his political supervisor should not be disturbed if the career civil servant calls attention to practical difficulties in the way of what the political executive wants to do. The career administrator must see and point out the weaknesses in all proposals no matter how great their appeal; and he also must find ways of carrying out administration policies when embodied in official decisions no matter how little they may appeal to him personally. He may interpret, but he must also respect the law in all of its substantive and procedural aspects. He brings to administration an understanding of those complications which although irritating are unavoidable in orderly and co-ordinated government. Finally, he is trained to see particular issues and immediate problems in relation to the general and broader requirements of the present and the future—to seek the balance of interests which is the continuous function of government. The sum of these traits is what constitutes his expertness.[5]

The Task Force was fully aware that many federal career executives do not resemble its model of the professional administrator with minimum emotional attachment to the policies of an administration and an unwillingness to participate in political affairs. Indeed, most bureau chiefs:

[4] *Ibid.*, p. 2, 3.
[5] *Ibid.*, pp. 3-4.

. . . have been more or less in the political arena. They have often had to "go up on the hill" alone, without much assistance from the secretary, to fight for their appropriations. They have had to go before legislative committees alone and argue the merits of legislative proposals. In these activities they were not merely supplementing the testimony of a secretary or assistant secretary by sitting at his elbow to provide data or details. They were carrying the main burden of testimony and argument. . . . Sometimes bureau chiefs have had to defend themselves against political attacks. They have at times taken the stump, not in election campaigns, but in campaigns to get support for programs. The hot issues often have not been handled in the departmental office but have been passed through quickly to the bureau chief.[6]

As the Task Force noted, the limitations of political executives thrust political activity upon career executives, many of whom are not reluctant to argue with congressmen for proposed legislation, plead for appropriations, defend the administration's position, make speeches on unsettled issues of public policy, work with interest groups, and generally fight the political battles of their bureaus and divisions. "Many bureau and division chiefs learned to be effective in the political role, and some relished the part."[7]

Rejection of the "Politically Neutral" Concept. Generally the Round Table found the Task Force description of career executives in operation to be accurate, but rejected its conception of the politically neutral career executive who remains out of all political activity. An executive who

[6] *Ibid.,* pp. 22-23.
[7] *Ibid.,* p. 5.

had been active in both political and career positions remarked:

> When one party dominates the country for twenty years,
> as the Democrats did, it is pretty easy for people who enter
> government service as careerists, as many of us here did, to
> drift into a political position unwittingly. As long as one
> party is dominant in both administration and Congress, the
> line between the career and the political executive never has
> to be drawn clearly. But we need to recognize that Congress
> fosters this. As someone said, if the political executive can-
> not answer the questions, Congress calls in the fellow who
> can, the careerist. If the careerist turns up a few years later
> with a new head of the department who is an appointee of
> the opposite political party, the same congressman may now
> regard the careerist as a politician who cannot be trusted.
> The executive who thought of himself as a careerist has
> suddenly become a political executive in the eyes of Con-
> gress. This shows that the executive branch alone cannot de-
> fine who is a career man and who is political. This is a two-
> way decision, and has to be made both on Capitol Hill and
> in the executive branch.

The Round Table found the portrait of the nonpolitical
career executive rather austere and unrealistic because
"every career executive is concerned with policy and political decisions day in and day out from the moment he
gets to be a grade 13. He cannot avoid these political
questions if he is to do his job properly." One executive
stated:

> You would not be able to recruit top executives for a
> strictly nonpolitical job. That kind of job is without flavor.
> It is not the sort of job that a man with spunk would live
> with, and he couldn't even if he wanted to. The facts of

life in Washington just wouldn't let him. The career executive must have policy commitments, and these commitments must be of the stature to attract and hold men of dedication and capacity.

Both the political and the career executives in the Round Table emphasized the "indigenous American tradition of the policy-committed career executive." A member concluded: "As a careerist, I am still a man of conscience. I reserve the right to have a conscience, to have my own beliefs and argue them in the proper places within the government." After all, as another member reminded the Round Table, "The principal in the Ministry of Health in Britain, who is supposed to be an impartial public servant, still has the tradition of believing in health even if he does not believe in the Labor Party or the Conservative Party."

While the Round Table found the Task Force's model of a career executive unrealistic in the federal political environment, it recognized that transient political executives tend to rely excessively on their career staffs to negotiate with legislative committees and interest groups:

> From time to time, we have all seen political executives who push their career people into politically exposed positions instead of taking the responsibility themselves for political defense of their program. The political executive owes it to his career people to consult them before crucial decisions are made so they have full opportunity to relate his decisions to the facts and experience available to the career staff. But he should be prepared to do the slugging on Capitol Hill and the public platform. Unfortunately, Congress won't have it this way. Congress will listen to the agency head who comes up to testify, but they really want the fellow down the line, especially if the boss is inexperienced, not too adept at testifying, or if something is wrong.

What the congressional committee wants is not a new secretary or assistant secretary as witness, but some Bill Smith who has been in the bureau a long time and really knows the program well.

A former executive agreed:

With all deference to the political executive, who comes and goes, he does not have the same familiarity with program as his career staff. Congress knows this and wants to get at the fellow who has the facts. But more than this, the public also has a right to hear from the fellow who really knows the operating experience of the program and can speak meaningfully about it.

Alleged Penalties of Political Involvement.   The Round Table did not share the conviction of the Task Force that career executives who publicly defended their programs before Congress necessarily lost their usefulness as administrators. As an experienced career executive recalled:

I have seen a lot of career executives dealing with Congress in the last quarter of a century. I cannot remember more than a half a dozen who got themselves in serious trouble because they did not know when to keep quiet and when to say to Congress that they were not instructed on a difficult political point. What is difficult about this situation is not that career people testify before committees. It is how they go up and the circumstances under which they testify.

Another career executive stated:

Inevitably, when a career executive has to carry the burden of testimony, some sensitive political issue is raised. I have never seen the time in thirteen years on this job that I could not say: "Well, that is a matter I will have to refer to the department. I cannot answer that." Usually a member of the department is at the hearing and will speak up, or else the committee calls in one of the political executives.

The extent to which a career executive becomes politically involved in congressional testimony depends partly on his skill in handling questions. For example, a career executive was asked by an appropriations subcommittee whether the budget he was defending in a particular area was adequate. He replied: "I want it distinctly understood that I am defending this budget estimate in spirit and in letter. We can do a good job with this budget." Whereupon the chairman turned to the career executive with some heat and said: "When I ask for your professional opinion, I expect an answer. I don't care what the department's opinion is. You are an expert on this matter; I want you to answer and you didn't."

The Round Table felt that the Task Force had exaggerated the penalties of political involvement.

> All of us career executives have testified on the Hill, and will continue to do so. When a clear line of policy has been laid down, and you are sent to the Hill to defend it, you do it. You are taking the words out of somebody else's mouth, so to speak, you are speaking for somebody else, but the fact remains that you do it. And nobody thinks badly of you for doing it. It is a derogatory commentary on career executives to assume that they do not have the capacity, desire, or willingness to defend their programs. They freqently do so, and often are by all odds better able to do it than many political executives.

Minimizing Political Involvement. On the other hand, the Round Table underlined the need for sensitive supervision by political executives of the relationships between career executives and Congress, particularly in minimizing contacts at lower levels in the civil service. A career executive noted:

> Both career and political executives can become careless in their political activities. In the latter months of the Truman administration, especially after the President announced that he would not run again, the White House staff neglected to fill some political posts in the departments and agencies on the theory that the jobs would not last long anyway. In this period, career executives became excessively involved in politics.

The problem of where to draw the line between the work of political and career executives is most difficult in the internal operations of the executive branch. Inevitably top career executives are involved in policy matters, and frequently their subordinates are also involved. Clearly, a competent career executive is expected by his political bosses to develop a sensitivity to issues in order to determine when an issue should be handled by political executives. As a political executive explained:

> A career man is not of much use to his boss unless he does that. You can easily make any of these issues political, but you do your boss a great disservice to burden him with all of them.

The line that the Task Force wanted to draw between political and career jobs represents an effort to impose some order upon an executive branch rich in variety and complicated by structural disorder. But its clear logic does not square with real life. Let me give you an example. The Forest Service today is looked upon as almost nonpartisan and nonpolitical. The Chief of the Forest Service has become a professional, although his job has as many political implications as any I know. Yet no one would tolerate seeing that post become a shifting political job. The job requires a career man of high professional qualifications and great political skill. We are more likely to find these qualities in a career man than in a political executive.

But if we need professionals to staff these positions, we also need men who develop a certain defensiveness in seeing that career people do not become excessively involved in political matters. There is a certain legal fiction in this whole area. We have to hold to it, or else we would be right back to the spoils system. If we did not have this myth of the nonpolitical professional administrator in many top posts today, we would be close to disaster. We cannot staff all the political positions required by the administration. If we are going to keep the government running, we have to live with the myth and propagate it.

HOW CAREER EXECUTIVES SPEND THEIR TIME

The career executives participating in the Round Table generally agreed that there were more variations in jobs within the career group than between those of political and career executives. The following descriptions by career executives of their jobs emphasize the range and diversity of functions. First, a career executive in a position comparable to that of an administrative assistant secretary, described his job this way:

A large percentage of my time is devoted to my function as staff officer to the secretary and under secretary. I have a relatively small staff—about 300 people. I spend perhaps a quarter of my time supervising the staff, and the other three quarters serving in a staff capacity to my bosses. I probably spend less than 5 per cent of my time with Congress, with industries, and other outside groups. I am mainly an intragovernmental man with occasional contacts with legislative staffs and members of the appropriations committees.

Second, a civil service bureau chief remarked:

I would like to endorse the view that there is more difference among career jobs than there is between my career
job and that of my immediate political boss, an assistant
secretary. The assistant secretary and I deal with the same
people and do many of the same sorts of things, but the
task of the assistant secretary is to keep me from losing
touch with the mass of the people, from becoming too in-
grown. The political executive provides that sensitivity to
the public pulse. He and I approach our similar jobs from
different angles. If we can learn to talk each other's language, we make a good team. Now, as to distribution of my
time, three fourths of it is spent not in internal activities
but in dealing with people outside of my own bureau. It
is all concerned with administration of the bureau's programs. I devote little time to the routine running of the
bureau. If I had to make a guess, I would estimate that
most of my time is spent in dealing with policies, controls,
and complaints. I probably have more direct contact with
members of Congress than most other bureau chiefs. These
contacts have been built up over many years, and Congress
fully expects the bureau chief to maintain the tradition. In
my experience, Congress has been getting into administrative matters increasingly so that my congressional contacts
keep increasing. My bureau has a lot of business with the
public. Consequently, many bills are proposed in Congress.
I think that in any bureau dealing with the public both the
political executive and the career executive are bound to
have a lot of contact with the people who use the bureau's
services.

Third, a career executive in one of the largest depart-

ments emphasized the importance of other factors that
condition the nature of his job:

My job is a hodge-podge of duties, and it varies from
one secretary to another. That is what makes it interesting.
Aside from my regular function of providing leadership,
what I do depends primarily on what my secretary wants
me to do. Many career executives devote a great deal of
time to the preparation and defense of budgets. In my
case, the budget task does not loom large in proportion to
other tasks. Many of our programs have been around for
about 150 years. They are no longer controversial and do
not raise many difficult questions of policy. My contacts lie
primarily in my department and in the Executive Branch,
perhaps 60 per cent in the department, 30 per cent in service agencies such as the General Services Administration,
General Accounting Office, Civil Service Commission, and
so forth, and 10 per cent on congressional matters.

Fourth, an executive in the top nonpolitical post in an
independent agency emphasized the theme of variety in
career positions.

I have had three different jobs in the course of the past
ten years. I am impressed with the vast differences in their
content, the nature of the principal contacts involved, and
the area of accountability. One job was a managerial one in
a large field activity. Here virtually 95 per cent of the job
was internal management of an industrial research plant.
In my second job I served as a senior assistant to a political
executive almost exclusively on a staff basis. Here the assignments dealt mainly with the internal management of a
huge department. In the third job, my time breaks down
very differently.

I would say that about 50 per cent of my time is devoted
to the internal management of the agency. This half of my

time breaks down into three general areas. The first is the program area, and includes the review, control, and stimulation of substantive projects with respect to the assigned responsibility of the agency. The second is personnel: selecting our own staff, and developing and working with key people in the organization. The third is financial management. This comprises the budget process, the distribution of funds, working with financial staffs, and so on.

About a quarter of my time is devoted to customer service within the executive branch, that is, in contacts with the agencies that utilize our services. . . . Probably not more than 5 per cent of my working day is devoted to congressional matters, and here my time is divided about equally between individual members and the staffs of the various committees. The balance, about 20 per cent, is devoted to work with outside groups—veterans groups, employee groups, professional societies, colleges and universities, individual citizens, and others. Typically these people seek us out. They come with a complaint, a problem, something to sell, a desire to improve their own status.

I try to control a certain amount of time to be devoted to development of program ideas. This is a sketch not of any one day but rather of how I have spent my time in the past year or so.

Fifth, a distinguished career executive with more than 30 years' experience in government service contrasted his job with those of other executives.

My job comprehends many of the things that have been discussed, but my work has some special features. I spend a lot of time on routine management, especially dealing with such service and regulating agencies as the Bureau of the Budget, the Civil Service Commission, the General Accounting Office, security staffs, and so forth. There are always questions arising with these agencies. You get one thing settled and another pops up in a different area. I also have my share of dealings with Congress. Let me give you an illustration.

This afternoon I was trying to resolve a difficult situation. We recently appointed to a training class in our service a number of Negroes. Some of our older officers took it upon themselves to make life rather hard for these appointees, and did a number of irritating things to discourage them from continuing in the class. We discovered who two of these troublemakers were. The question was: what should we do with them? Should we suspend them or not? In the midst of our consideration, an influential member of Congress called to state his views on just how far we should go in disciplining those people. Here was a typical personnel problem involving congressional interest. Don't ask me how I resolved the matter. I haven't done so yet.

Some of my activity is not too common in the federal service. For instance, my work brings me into contact with the judicial branch of the government. I get requests from court officers for information on particular cases, diagnoses of certain matters, and similar things. In addition, I have a certain number of contacts with business stemming from the manufacturing business connected with my bureau. We do several million dollars worth of business each year, and have a lot of technical problems common to industry.

I have to spend some of my time getting across the government's views to the special constituencies interested in our work. This involves the drafting of speeches and the writing of articles usually for technical journals of one kind or another. I have to deal with certain groups interested in special aspects of the bureau's programs. This kind of work is very important and one that some executives tend to neglect or to minimize.

I don't know how to estimate the time I devote to congressional business. We have to make reports on hundreds of individual bills that affect us directly or indirectly, and that takes a lot of time. If I add in the time spent on appropriations and contacts with individual congressmen, it might add up to about 15 per cent. The bureau has a sort of watchdog committee in the Senate, and we maintain close touch with the members. They visit us; we refer problems to them, and so on. Frankly, I am very happy to have such a committee. They have been of tremendous help to us because they have become acquainted with our problems and have in no sense been an irritant or handicap. There is no House counterpart of the Senate committee but one of the House committee chairmen takes a good deal of interest in what we do. He calls me over now and then to find out what is going on or what we want done on a particular bill. I appear perhaps once or twice a month before some committee on the Hill.

Sixth, a former government executive participating in the discussions recalled some valuable advice he received as a new bureau chief in a major department:

I remember what a highly successful bureau chief told me at lunch one day. He said: "If you are one of these career fellows who looks at Congress as something strange and far away and something you ought to be afraid of, you are never going to make the grade in your job." He told me that he spends time with Congress and individual members not only in official business during working hours but also in the evenings, at dinner, and so on. He impressed me as a career executive who had developed a very realistic and thorough knowledge of congressional behavior. In addition, he had a gift for keeping in touch with the people in field installations who worked under his general supervision and with the people his program served. These relationships, he told me, provided a human contact that helped to keep him pretty well adjusted. He felt strongly that one of the important requisites for an effective executive career is emotional balance.

He also devoted a fair amount of time to developing support and understanding for his program among opinion groups in the country: churches, service clubs, various civic organizations. He reported that he was often called upon for help by state officials who wanted assistance on some technical or professional problem like planning a new institution or selecting new personnel. He regarded assistance to states as an important part of his job, not only because constructive assistance helped to develop high prestige for the federal service but also because it promoted a professional cooperation between levels of government that was frequently very helpful to the federal bureau.

Seventh, another Round Table participant continued the theme of diversity in career positions:

My activity has to do principally with legislative matters. Some of the things I do are strikingly similar to the functions of other career executives, but others are almost unique in the federal service. One of the most rewarding things I do is meeting and talking with college groups, newspaper reporters, and other groups interested in the procedures and techniques of government. About 10 per cent of my time is spent largely over the telephone and strictly on a nonpartisan basis with members of Congress, the calendar committees of the parties, and other individuals interested in particular legislative proposals. Another 10 per cent of my time is given over to my staff and other people in the bureau who work with me.

About 25 per cent of my time is devoted to the various governmental agencies and their staffs who come in to discuss their legislative problems. This is by all odds the most difficult part of the job. If I allowed my staff or the agencies to control my time, I would be spending all day every day in meetings. At least an additional 25 per cent consists of staff work for the White House on executive orders, bills, and various legislative matters. The remaining quarter of my time is spent on internal matters in the bureau.

My job deals mainly with political matters in which decisions have to be made by political executives. The challenge is to remain a career executive while under constant pressure to mind somebody else's business in the political sphere. The only way I can protect myself from stepping over the line into a political operation is to be acutely sensitive to political problems. My major defense against going over the line is the realization that the President expects this office to be institutional rather than political. We would be letting the President down if we started making political decisions.

My job illustrates the difficulty in trying to draw a sharp distinction between political and career executive positions in terms of "political involvement." I get "involved" in political matters not to provide political leadership in resolving political issues but rather to help to clarify the political issues for resolution by political executives. Part of my job consists of keeping issues unresolved until contending positions have been clarified and the necessary information has been analyzed. Career executives have to expose themselves to political problems without becoming political themselves. This is a continuous process that has its own rewards and frustrations.

I don't know whether my job can be compared to the other career jobs described here, but the essential element in my job is the realization that my primary function is to see that in the area in which I work the President gets good staff work. This is a sufficiently lofty goal to keep a career man pretty humble. I cannot divorce myself except for fleeting moments from the overhanging shadow of the oval room in the White House.

Very rarely does my office make policy decisions in default of decision making by political executives. When this occurs, I run for cover as fast as I can and simply tell my political superiors that events overtook me, that it seemed to me that the weight of evidence was in the direction of doing this or that, and that I had done it. But I could not go on from day to day in a policy vacuum. It just wouldn't work. Instead of making decisions myself, my job is to mobilize all the resources I can in the bureau and in other agencies to withhold the pressure for a decision until the problem has been satisfactorily resolved. I am supposed to get the issues focussed sharply enough to merit White House consideration.

As a career executive I have appeared from time to time before congressional committees, particularly to sound out congressional attitudes on matters on which the administration has not yet taken a firm position. I am a hardy defender of the opportunity I have had to be an administration scout before Congress. It is never a wholly comfortable role, but I think it is an appropriate role for a career man to fill.

The Round Table discussions suggested that career executives, on the whole, talk somewhat more freely about their jobs than political executives do about theirs. No doubt many factors help to account for the relatively greater verbal facility of the career executive, but two significant factors are the familiarity of the career man with the political environment and his professional interest in governmental service for career purposes.

THE NEED FOR POLITICAL SKILL

As the Round Table discussions stressed, the most important element common to high career executive jobs is involvement in policy. Moreover, this element makes it very difficult to separate the work of the career executive sharply from that of the political executive.

The Value of Experience.   One executive advanced the view that career executives often have greater political skill than do political executives:

> Top-side government jobs have a great deal in common, whether they are career or political. We tend to overdraw the distinction between career and non-career executives. Perhaps one might say that the distinction between the two groups lies not in the nature of their jobs but rather in the degree of political experience each possesses. . . . No single type of government executive has a monopoly on political experience and sensitivity, but the long-time career executive easily outranks the transient political executive of limited tenure in political skill. A career executive who has been on the job for 25 years or so in Washington is a master of something that the rest of us would be rank amateurs at.

Another executive agreed:

> It would be better if both the political appointees and the career officials clearly recognized that both groups are in governmental service together. Some are here for a little while and some are here maybe for a life-time career. What unites them in the same kind of enterprise is their involvement in public policy and in trying to run an agency of a government in which both Congress and the President exercise a great deal of influence and power.

The Round Table repeatedly emphasized the importance of personality and individual characteristics in assessing the relationships of career executives to their political superiors and to Congress.

If you are dealing with Congress, as most of us do, a great deal depends on whether you are able to convince the committees of your reliability and dependability. It does not matter really whether you are political or career. What matters more is whether you have the confidence of the committee. If you have it, then you can do business effectively. It is the personal equation that is crucial. But it takes time to discover with which congressman or secretary it is possible to develop an effective relationship.

A former executive added:

This is a kind of expertness that the career executive gradually develops. On the other hand, the political executive often does not have it. At the outset the political executive usually lacks political contacts not only with members of Congress but also with colleagues in the executive branch, interdepartmental committees, service and control agencies that work for the President, and the constituency groups affected by the program of a particular agency.

Another executive said:

The contrast between political and career executives in political experience is especially delicate when a new administration takes office. Then the career people have it all over the political appointees. This may cause political executives to resent the career people upon whom they have to rely for continuity of knowledge and expert skill in operating in a strange environment.

Relationships Between Political and Career Executives. Members of the Round Table agreed that really skillful political executives know how to use their top career staff without being easily offended or unduly sensitive. "The best thing for the political executive to do is to work closely with his career executives, appreciate them fully, and thank God every night for having them around," said a relatively new political executive. "But at the same time, the political executive has to retain sufficient independence so he does not become a captive of the permanent staff."

From the point of view of the career executive, the problem is to learn to respect and value his political boss without seeking to dominate him.

In a so-called old-line agency, a new political executive frequently feels that the scope of his initiative in dealing with policy matters is very narrow. As such an executive said:

> One thing that has impressed me the most is the relatively small area where the political executive can really make policy, compared to the policy roles of Congress on one side and the career executives on the other. The career fellow appears to make more policy than the political executive does. He can operate rather freely in areas where the policy issues are not sufficiently significant to merit the attention of the political executive. On the other hand, the political executive is often faced by a career staff ready to veto one of his policy proposals. I don't know how many times I have been told by a career executive: "What you propose here is absolutely sound, but on the Hill it will be murder because of this or that, and, anyway, somebody tried the same thing ten years ago, and look what happened to them."
>
> I think it is quite true that unless an executive has been in Washington a number of years, he does not develop the sensitivity to the way certain things are likely to be received by Congress, the general public, or special interest groups. Nothing in previous business experience is likely to be of much use to the political executive in developing these political skills.

As quoted comments indicate, the Round Table veered strongly to the position that career executives supplied not only managerial competence, expert knowledge of government administration, and detailed understanding of the development and background of programs and issues but also a political skill that political executives sometimes lacked in adequate measure. Career executives participating in the Round Table took the position that it would be devastating to have secretaries, under secretaries, and assistant secretaries flanked only by subordinate political executives. They were alarmed by the probable consequences of a situation in which top political executives dealt primarily with subordinates who were also transient amateurs in the arts and special skills of public management. At the same time, the career executives believed strongly that a political executive ought to have some freedom in changing career executives:

> With a new administration coming in, it is only fair for career executives to inform their political superior that if he was not satisfied with them, he would not have to go through the business of fighting the civil service statutes and regulations to get them out of their jobs. Instead, they would resign.

One participant has occupied a career position since its establishment several years ago. When asked by an under secretary of the department what civil service protection he had in the job, he replied: "Simply this. As long as I can serve here to the satisfaction of the secretary and the under secretary, I am here. When my services are no longer useful, I get out." He added:

> As long as the career fellow looks at his job that way, he

can serve effectively. If he looks at it any other way, he soon goes out of business. Maybe the civil service laws give him some protection in retaining that job, but his own code of behavior calls upon him to resign when he loses the confidence of his superiors. Maybe this forces the career man to put his job, and maybe his career, on the line, but in the long run, it works much better this way for all concerned.

One significant theme developed by the Round Table was that the career executive can be very helpful in protecting the political executive against political hazards. A career bureau chief observed:

> The able career man can be useful in standing between the political executive and Congress, just as the able political executive can protect his career men from political attack. This may be a job for the career executive that the Hoover Commission deplored; nevertheless it will remain important so long as relatively inexperienced political executives come and go so rapidly in Washington.

Another career executive stated:

> It has been my experience that one of the most frustrating things that can happen to a career man is to feel that he has more political sensitivity than the political appointee who directs him. A political appointee does not necessarily have political acuteness.

Another added that "one of the most disappointing experiences any career man has is to be told by his boss that he just doesn't understand politics."

On balance, the Round Table discussion supported the conclusions about the federal career executive that had been reached by a prominent management consultant in 1957:

Actually, large numbers of bureau chiefs cannot avoid making policy or carrying political responsibility. The real trick is to work conscientiously to promote the political policies of the party in power, both parties being presumed to operate in the public interest. Most career executives are better politicians—in the best sense of the word—than are their political supervisors. The present administration talked a good deal about a Washington housecleaning in the early months of the first term. While political appointees were changed, and properly, few significant changes were made in the career service. This is not a failure on the part of the administration but rather is evidence that a large number of permanent professionals must be in important posts if our government is to function.[8]

[8] Richard M. Paget, "Strengthening the Federal Career Executive," *Public Administration Review*, Vol. 17 (Spring 1957), p. 93.

IV

The Political Setting:
The Executive Branch

A COMPLEX OF FORCES and counter-forces influences the setting in which the federal executive works. In this chapter, factors that arise from the environment of the executive branch are discussed. In later chapters, such external influences as the Congress, political parties, and special interest groups are considered.

PRESIDENTIAL MANAGEMENT

Generalization about American political relationships is difficult because the environment is dynamic and personal ties are important. Congress, for example, "is no fixed entity—it is a group of human beings reshuffled at regular intervals by popular elections and shifted daily, even hourly, as different issues evoke varying reactions in the minds of individual members."[1] Similarly, "the presidency is an office so colored by the personality of the incumbent and so affected by the current of the times that beyond the formal legal attributes of the position tremendous scope for self-expression remains."[2] In the same way, the rela-

[1] E. Pendleton Herring, *Presidential Leadership* (1940), p. 135.
[2] *Ibid.*, pp. 135-36.

tionships between the President and his immediate staff on the one hand and the heads of executive agencies on the other vary with the character and personality of the individuals involved and the pressures and imperatives of the day.

President Eisenhower's illnesses, beginning in 1955, dramatized one familiar, yet salient feature of the presidential office: its crushing burden. During most of the nineteenth century the President was able to discharge his duties with the help of no more than a handful of clerks, and his work consisted mainly of routine housekeeping chores that belied the significance of the office. But today, when the President serves as leader of the free world, head of a complicated set of alliances, promoter and manager of a stable and prosperous economy, spokesman of a faceless majority and interpreter of its social needs, and commander of the forces of defense and security, he requires a staff of about 1,300 to assist him in the Executive Office of the President.[3]

While the presidency is the apex of the executive branch as well as of the national political structure, the organization of the executive branch is not symmetrical. Authority does not necessarily follow a clearly delineated line running from a broad pyramidal base common to all agencies upward to the White House. As Lindsay Rogers once stated:

> . . . throughout much of the administrative field, the President is unable to initiate or to prevent. The heads of

[3] In June 1958, the Executive Office of the President comprised: the White House Office, 394; the Bureau of the Budget, 440; the Council of Economic Advisers, 28; the National Security Council, 64; the Office of Defense Mobilization, 251; and the President's Advisory Committee on Government Organization, 6. The staff of the Executive Mansion and Grounds was 72.

departments and independent establishments have authority which is theirs to use without the necessity of securing
presidential approval.[4]

As administrator-in-chief of the national government, the
President stands generally accountable for the whole executive establishment even though he lacks control over
many of its parts.

Presidential Unity vs. Agency Autonomy. From his
vantage point at the summit, the President's aim is to
establish workable government-wide standards that will
foster uniformity in the conduct of government agencies.
The President and his staff endeavor to prescribe general
policies to guide the heads of agencies, and to create and
operate facilities that help co-ordinate various governmental programs, make information available to the President on a timely basis, and tap the resources of the executive branch for the imaginative formulation of policy.
Agency heads and their principal deputies and assistants,
however, have an inherent drive toward greater operating
autonomy even though they face the same problems of co-
ordination and control over their bureaus and divisions
that the President faces in his relationships to them.

An executive who joined the Eisenhower administration
early in 1953 observed the reaction of colleagues who were
overwhelmed with the complexity and newness of the
governmental job.

> The average presidential appointee sat in his new office
> trying to avoid an early knock-out. He asked himself:
> "How can I survive in this jungle that no one has properly
> described to me before my arrival?" And he decided that

[4] Lindsay Rogers, "The American Presidential System," *Political Quarterly*, Vol. 8 (October 1937), pp. 524-25.

he was invited to become an executive in the new administration because of the skills and knowledge that he had
acquired in industry and elsewhere.

What he wanted above all was to be allowed to operate
in the way he knew best. He pleaded: "Let me alone, and
I'll give you accomplishment and action. That is what you
are going to reward me for, not for co-ordination and all
these things that lead mainly to inaction and frustration."
He pictured himself caught in a responsibility that he was
unable to discharge because of the restrictions and conflicts
that obstructed his freedom of action.

The conflict between the new executive and the presidential co-ordinators goes beyond personal differences.
There is almost an inevitable rivalry between the people
who are trying to get a job done in an environment in
whose mysteries they have not been trained and the President's staff who are trying to develop a standard, rational
approach throughout the government. The first instinct of
the executive is to stretch his operating autonomy.

Executives experienced in governmental administration
usually learn to live on more or less comfortable terms with
the President's staff. Occasionally the executives in a department are happy to rely on the support of the President's men in disciplining a powerful bureau. A former
Defense Department executive noted that:

> The Defense Department is a superstructure on top of
> three operating agencies. It is often very difficult for the
> Secretary of Defense to resist the powerful pressures gen-
> erated by military and civilian staffs in his constituent agen-
> cies. He may be able to be more effective in his job if he
> occasionally gives a questionable matter his tacit approval
> in the hope that the President's staff in the Bureau of the
> Budget or elsewhere may do what the secretary wants to
> achieve, but cannot do himself. The presidential agencies

can be tough; they can interfere with and even usurp departmental functions; but in many pressure situations, the departmental executive has to rely on them to survive.

From the point of view of departmental executives, presidential control is exercised through a double chain of command. One runs through the secretaries and other agency heads while the other runs through the presidential agencies and White House aides. Since the 1930's, the latter have increased substantially, and notable progress in presidential management has been achieved, especially in the development of budget policy and administration and in economic analysis.

The President's ability to direct and control his administration has also been strengthened by reorganization plans reducing the number of executive agencies by incorporating them into existing ones or into new ones. Some of the principal proposals of the first Hoover Commission in 1949 dealt with the regrouping of government activities into major departments and agencies under the President and the concentration of authority and responsibility in department heads. Since 1949, powers formerly vested by law in bureau chiefs have been largely transferred to department heads in the departments of the Treasury, Justice, Post Office, Interior, Agriculture, Commerce, and Labor. Since 1947, the authority of the Secretary of Defense to manage the three military departments has been somewhat strengthened by legislation. While new agencies and functions tend to replace old ones, various reorganizing efforts have succeeded in simplifying the executive structure. As a Task Force of the second Hoover Commission observed:

> The persistence of these efforts, going back more than 40 years, to simplify and strengthen the departments under

the Chief Executive, is recognition of the vitality of the
constitutional principle that the departments are the main-
stay of the President's executive function, and that departmental management is the critical element in integrated
operation of the executive branch.[5]

As the second Hoover Commission pointedly observed,
improvements in presidential management had not been
matched by comparable increases in the capacity of agency
heads to manage their bureaus effectively. From their relatively weak managerial position, agency heads and deputies
may regard the President's staff as natural enemies rather
than allies in their struggle against the operating autonomy
of the bureaus.

The Eisenhower Cabinet. The Eisenhower administration endeavored to transform the cabinet into an important instrument of presidential co-ordination. In cabinet
sessions, department heads and other key executives have
played a major advisory role in charting public policy and
recommending decisions. While the cabinet has been
utilized more by President Eisenhower than by many of
his immediate predecessors, its impact upon federal executives is not entirely clear. For example, one observer
noted:

> The cabinet is a collection of people with very little in
> common, whose individual effectiveness depends on their
> personal force. It has not been a match for the National
> Security Council, which is a supercabinet committee, or the
> other devices that have been set up to keep pace with the
> changing needs of government.

[5] U.S. Commission on Organization of the Executive Branch of the
Government, *Task Force Report on Personnel and Civil Service* (1955),
p. 13.

Another observer said "the new cabinet is an organization in which the number of voices is about equally divided between secretaries and other officials. The non-secretarial voices seem to be more articulate, and they are more accustomed to winning verbal battles."

A third observer noted that there has been more systematic use of the cabinet in this administration.

> It has an elaborate machinery headed by a cabinet operations officer who prepares agenda, follows up in detail on decisions, and makes the members come whether they want to or not. I think you have to go all the way back to President Benjamin Harrison to find comparable use of the cabinet. Both Harrison and Eisenhower may have been impressed by the cabinet as an instrument of government because of their experience as military staff officers.

A fourth observer pointed out that the Eisenhower cabinet may be in difficulty because "the President has allowed too many issues to be taken into the cabinet for discussion. Some of them are insignificant and merely fill up the agenda. But a lot of topics on the agenda are of primary concern only to one department, which gets unhappy when a score or more people around the cabinet table pontificate on that subject."

It is doubtful that the Eisenhower administration has realized the full potentialities of the cabinet. Current evidence has not forced a modification of the familiar conclusion that "It is hardly an exaggeration . . . to say that for decades hard-driving heads of busy departments have been cynical to the point of resenting cabinet meetings as a waste of time."[6]

---

[6] Arthur W. Macmahon and John D. Millett, *Federal Administrators* (1939), p. 5.

IMPACT OF PRESIDENTIAL STAFFING

A distinctive characteristic of the executive branch today is the continuing communication between the examiners of the Bureau of the Budget and departmental budget officers; between the President's press secretary and departmental information officers; between the Civil Service Commission and departmental personnel officers; and so on. How do these functional relationships affect agency heads? How much of an executive's responsibility is diluted by presidential staffing?

There is ample evidence that some agency heads defer weakly, while others stoutly resist, the activities of presidential staffs. Resistance to presidential co-ordination may range from personal appeals by an agency head directly to the President to vigorous competition between presidential and departmental staffs in formulating and defending their respective positions.

Institutional and Personal Aspects of Executive Office. Some light may be cast on presidential-agency relations by distinguishing between the institutional and personal aspects of executive office. As one career executive explained:

> The institution of the presidency is defined by the Constitution and a host of statutes. It has no flesh and blood individual in it. By the same token the secretary of a department is also an institution with no flesh and blood individual in it, a deposit of organic statutes and administrative tradition.
>
> But contrast the institution with the personal side of the executive office. We all know that the operation of any executive office is molded by its occupant. One of the pre-

occupations of the career executive is the effort to blend into a harmonious whole the secretary as the embodiment of executive authority and as presidential adviser and political party representative. The agency head is personally responsible for his agency's activities and for interpreting the law and the agency's powers under the law. But he is also the impersonal institution of executive office. The permanent staff will probably try to emphasize the institutional rather than the personal aspects of the executive function, but there is bound to be some conflict because people are people, and they don't like to lose their personality by becoming institutional.

Occasionally the power and personal force of an executive have been strong enough to transcend institutional arrangements. Harold Ickes, as Secretary of the Interior, was usually able to get what he wanted directly from the President, despite opposition from presidential co-ordinators. In his case, personal capacity supplemented the secretary's institutional role as the authoritative representative of his department. Some agency heads have minimized the institutional effectiveness of their office by relying excessively on personal influence with the President. Newly-appointed agency heads seem to emphasize their personal relationship to the President while experienced career executives are usually much more aware of the institutional dimensions of executive office.

The impact of presidential staffs upon departmental staffs is likely to be only as great as the secretary and under secretary permit. The leverage that the agency executives can exercise is the product of their personal force and competence and the institutional facilities at their command. The success of many executives may lie partly in their skill in maintaining points of support and developing co-operative responses in the presidential establishment and elsewhere, and partly in their ability to retain a measure of agency autonomy by surmounting the restrictive standard operating procedures which are the stock-in-trade of presidential agencies.

The Budget Process. The Bureau of the Budget, the oldest presidential agency, generally has a high standing with agency executives. One executive reported:

> I think the Budget Bureau has done an excellent job. We have had almost no trouble in justifying what we need through the budget process, and where we have had disagreements, we have usually gone to the Director of the Budget and settled our differences calmly. By and large the Bureau has not been tough enough on our agency. But this is a personal view based on a conviction that we need to economize.

Another executive indicated that the Bureau has aided his agency by developing and analyzing its budget justifications. "Its review enables us to do a better job before the appropriations committees. The Bureau helps us to express our position in a more logical and better manner. It gives us good practice in justifying what we ask for."

An executive of the Defense Department noted that the role of the Bureau of the Budget is flexible:

> Many times the Bureau really does not know what is in our budget until it hits Congress. It is an enormous budget, and it is prepared about 18 months before the beginning of the fiscal year. Hence many necessary changes in the budget have to be made. The Budget Bureau deals with this budget not so much through the regular review process but more through the apportionment system. Instead of trying to determine whether our long-range estimates are sound, the

Bureau deals rather with current realities by apportioning funds during the fiscal year for a few months at a time. This system works rather well, although it does pinch the departments at times.

A perennial question facing agency executives is whether any budget submitted to Congress should lack a bargaining element. One executive explained the problem:

> Part of the operating philosophy of many executives is to include in their budget estimates enough money in the beginning to be able to compromise with the President's staff and Congress and still come out with what the agency wants. An alternative approach is to include in the estimates only what the agency really needs and to fight for that estimate to the last step. The latter position may be dangerous to the bureau chief. When the budget emerges from the machinery of central departmental review and analysis by the Budget Bureau, his budget is very tight. If Congress cuts it further, the bureau's program may have to be curtailed.

Another executive agreed:

> We have never been able to convince the Budget Bureau that there ought to be a little fat in there so that Congress can cut the budget and still leave us enough to carry on necessary operations. The career executives with long experience in federal finance try to leave some extras in their estimates for protection, while the tendency of the new political executive is to submit an "honest" budget. From the standpoint of practical politics, it is probably better to have a bargaining budget.

A nonfederal executive inquired whether an executive newly-recruited from business is more likely to submit a tight budget:

Do you whittle down your budget leaving little room for bargaining purposes on the theory that you are using a practice commonly employed in industry, namely, that you put before the board of directors a tight budget and you expect the board to understand it in those terms and approve it without reductions? Do you feel that this business practice is based on a principle that is worth defending even though you lose in its defense, or do you think that you can bring Congress around to the view of facing your estimates as honest ones that will not bear pruning without harming particular programs?

A federal executive with many years' experience in business replied:

I think we are all motivated by our backgrounds. We had to have honest budgets in business. When we got dishonest budgets, we fired the people as untrustworthy. You could not have a satisfactory operation without a firm budget. For that reason I find it hard to trust government people who prepare inflated budgets. After a few years in Washington I still maintain that the bargaining elements in a budget estimate ought to be minimized. Our department has not been badly hurt on the Hill, despite the tightness of the budget estimates, but some of the bureaus in the department probably would not agree with me.

The impact of presidential staffing upon agency heads and their deputies is neither uniform throughout the executive branch nor clearly defined. Much depends upon the agency itself: how well-established or controversial its programs may be, its relations with key congressional committees, the intensity of interest group concern in its programs, its capacity for effective, uncorrupted administration, and its ability to recruit able staff. Over and above these institutional factors stands the personal equation of the personality and talents of agency executives.

The Civil Service Commission. Central personnel administration is normally more troublesome to federal executives than the co-ordinating services under the President's general management. Personnel controls appear to dig more deeply into and to bind more tightly the discretionary authority of departmental executives.

Opposition by executives to the activities of the Civil Service Commission stems from many sources, but three major factors stand out. First, the Civil Service Commission is charged with the responsibility of administering a myriad of statutes that prescribe in detail how the federal personnel system should operate in order to keep rascals and unfit persons out of government jobs. As the policeman guarding the integrity of federal employment, the Commission has succeeded in keeping out the old-fashioned spoilsman and the incompetent but at the price of hemming in the line operator with restrictive rules governing job classification, appointment, promotion, transfer, salary change, and dismissal of employees.

Second, many of the restrictive rules administered by the Commission have been required by mandatory legislation obtained directly by veterans' lobbies. The Commission's role with respect to veterans' preference and similar provisions is not merely that of policeman; it is also an agency at the service of a clientele group. This is probably one of the least understood aspects of the Washington environment for new executives.

Third, the central personnel agency restricts the operating freedom of executives in routine administration where their counterparts outside of government are more or less unrestricted. As a former business executive now in government stated:

> I think most executives out of business expected when they came to Washington to face a Bureau of the Budget or some similar group. They were used to justifying their proposed budgets to a tough finance committee or board of directors. But it was a new experience to hold an agency head responsible for the operation of his agency and yet deny him a measure of freedom in ordinary personnel administration.

The imprecise status of the Civil Service Commission complicates its relationship to other agencies. As presently constituted, it functions as a staff agency for three-score departments and agencies in the executive branch, but it stands outside the presidential establishment. Moreover, it administers a long list of statutes for whose operation it is answerable to Congress. One observer stated:

> About a decade or more ago, we used to ask around Washington, "For whom does the Civil Service Commission work?" We used to reply, "Well, we think it works first for its congressional committees, second for the status employees, third for the American Legion in support of veterans' preference laws, fourth for the civil service employees unions, and possibly fifth for the President." Since the end of World War II, the President has moved up in this list but it is difficult to tell just how far.

In recent years the Civil Service Commission has attempted to delegate to the agencies the actual administration of many statutory programs. A former executive of the Commission stated:

> The whole thesis of the Commission today is that there should be as extensive a delegation as is possible under the

law. There should be greater discretion on the part of agency management within the framework of broad personnel policy, and every possible administrative and legislative step should be taken to achieve these ends. But there has to be an occasional check to see whether these delegated powers are effectively used. No matter how much delegation is achieved, the Commission is still held responsible by Congress for effective administration of the personnel statutes.

The inspection services established by the Commission to evaluate agency personnel programs have been attacked as unwarranted interference with agency administration. One executive reported:

> Some of the Commission's staff have told local managers of our field offices that they have poor personnel programs, inadequate employee training, no coffee break, insufficient emphasis on incentive awards, and so on. The Commission can stir up a lot of employee criticism this way and interfere with administration.

Another executive reported a similar field office problem:

> Civil service inspectors have interviewed field personnel at lower salary levels, asking about the administration of personnel programs. They raise questions in the minds of employees. If there is an effective union, soon it is charging that we are treating the employees unfairly and not complying with some civil service law. If we are violating a personnel statute, the Commission should so inform the head of the agency, but it should not be stirring up trouble between the agency and its field staffs.

The Commission was defended by another departmental executive, who reported:

> The inspection service of the Commission has improved

a great deal, although it surely has interfered with some elements that are strictly the business of the agency's managers. Nevertheless, these inspections can often be helpful to the agency that is doing a better personnel job. One of our bureaus that had a great deal of difficulty in handling personnel matters because of its own defects and mistakes had much of its personnel authority withdrawn. I don't believe that our top departmental staff would have regained full confidence in the bureau's handling of its personnel had it not been for the series of reports made by the inspection staff of the Commission that personnel administration in the bureau was getting progressively stronger. From that standpoint, the Commission was a great help to the department.

INTERAGENCY RIVALRIES

The federal executive operates in a complex of agencies, each of which has been added piecemeal to the executive branch. Each agency develops its own bureaucratic organization and administrative traditions. Rarely is a single agency a wholly self-contained unit whose jurisdiction neither conflicts nor overlaps with that of another agency. The great range of powers and authority conferred upon the executive branch must be shared by agencies that have their own statutory bases, motivating values and historical traditions. A single agency thus can do little without dipping into the affairs of other agencies. A federal executive can scarcely mind his own business without minding someone else's as well.

It is difficult to exaggerate the importance of interagency relations in an executive's environment. Contacts between agencies absorb a great deal of his time, but an agency head normally has only a few assistants experienced in handling complex interagency matters. If he expects to survive or to be effective, the executive must develop sensitivity to the interagency aspects of his work. He requires patience, an ability to endure long sessions of reasoning with others, and a capacity to survive many meetings and consultations in a turbulent atmosphere.

Some Classic Cases. Some instances of interagency rivalry are classic: the Army Engineers and the Bureau of Reclamation, the Treasury Department and the Federal Reserve Board, the Soil Conservation Service and the Agricultural Extension Service, the Forest Service and the former Grazing Service, and the rivalries of the Air Force, the Army, the Navy, and the Marine Corps. Others may be less well-known but nonetheless significant, for example, the dispute between the Department of Commerce and the Interstate Commerce Commission over competitive rates in the transportation industries, and the conflict between the Departments of Labor and of Health, Education, and Welfare over the inclusion of labor standards in federal grant-in-aid programs.

In recent years the most significant interagency rivalry has concerned the three military departments. During more than a decade of unification under the National Security Act of 1947, competition among the military departments remained an essential feature of defense organization. Rivalry in the formulation and support of budgetary proposals carries through to the development of weapons and weapons systems. Occasionally the competitive struggle for technological superiority gets out of hand and leads to court martials. On the other hand, competition may be conducive to higher levels of performance. Many executives believe that some measure of interagency competition is healthy provided it is not carried to extremes, but the proper degree of competition and the appropriate methods of preventing "unfair" competition are matters of dispute.

Discovering the Public Interest. Does interagency rivalry help executives to discover the public interest in a controversial area of public policy? Most executives believe that the nature of the public interest is illuminated by debate and competition, but some believe that better results may be achieved at less cost through the cultivation of co-operation and co-ordination among agencies. Generally the modern literature of public administration has extolled the virtues of unity, rationality, and integration rather than conflict and separatism.

The traditional view was expressed by an executive with extensive experience in directing programs of economic mobilization:

> Interagency rivalry certainly is one way to discover the public interest, but the rivalry ought to be resolved within the executive branch. Executives need to be refreshed by the cross-fertilization of conflicting ideas on where the public interest lies, but this objective can be accomplished better by gathering together officials from various departments who have a common problem to discuss. For example, if the Forest Service and the Grazing Service have differences in policy, I would be inclined to preserve their competitive existence but I would somehow bring them together in order to compromise their differences within the executive branch.

The case for interagency rivalry is substantial. In the first place, as one participant stated: "Whatever disservice competition does to administrators and whatever difficulties it imposes on them, it is often the only possible way to resolve an issue." In areas where powerful agencies have staked out unassailable claims the cost of continuing conflict may be sufficiently high to make a resolution of the controversy imperative.

Second, as an executive asserted:

> Frequent explosions inside an administration can be very healthy. They are an essential ingredient of opinion making in a democracy. They dramatize policy conflicts, spotlight areas of costly duplication of services, and create interest in governmental activities.

Third, competition in government, like competition in business enterprise, may keep government executives more alert, more imaginative, and more vigorous. It is claimed that the settlement of policy conflicts among rival agencies tends to produce a more positive agreement, whereas co-ordination of the activities of interested parties usually leads to a less imaginative conclusion with a "lower common denominator."

Perhaps the main argument against rivalry is that it is difficult to control and may perpetuate itself. When interagency rivalry gets out of hand, as it seems in the case of the Army Engineers and the Bureau of Reclamation in the field of water resources, the country may pay a high price in waste of resources, confusion of responsibility, and failure to obtain optimum benefits from the expenditure of federal funds.

Adjusting Interagency Conflicts.   Whether competition or co-ordination is favored, at some point a settlement must ordinarily be reached. How far down the bureaucratic ladder should executives go in working out a settlement? According to an experienced executive:

In dealing with legislative proposals affecting two or more agencies, if specific or technical program issues are involved, it is desirable to consult the technicians—the career men who have grown up with a particular job. Try to find two technicians who will talk to each other. Chances are that agency differences can be brought sharply into focus this way.

For example, there may be a proposal to raise the grazing fee in the national forests from 15 cents to 30 cents an animal. In order to tackle this issue properly it is essential to talk with the men who have been out in the grazing areas of the national forests who know the ground, how much grass grows on it, what the rainfall is, how many acres it takes to feed an animal, and how many sheepherders there will be.

On the other hand, if the legislative proposal charts a new policy or deals with the philosophy of a program, it is usually better to begin interagency discussions at the highest possible levels. In such matters, it is usually wise to let the technicians alone. They don't want to stick their necks out on a matter of high policy. In any case what is needed is not clarification of departmental positions but some clear thinking about the broad implications of the proposals.

Presidential habits affect the intensity and timing of interagency disputes. President Franklin D. Roosevelt rather thrived on conflict among his executives. He preferred often to be confronted directly by rival convictions and positions, and used them to sharpen his own thinking. In contrast, President Eisenhower relies heavily upon coordinating devices to minimize conflict.

One factor that encourages executives to resolve their interagency differences is the fear that unresolved differences will be carried to the cabinet. One career bureau chief stated:

If somebody above you in the hierarchy gives you a hard look and says, "If you fellows don't get together, this problem will go to the cabinet and you know what will happen then," you will buckle down and come up with something because a cabinet decision might turn out to be bad.

British experience during World War II was similar. An executive recalled:

The wartime cabinet secretariat was composed of the permanent under secretaries of nine key ministries and a working group made up of representatives of these ministries who worked closely with their cabinet officers. These men more or less lived together during the war. Most of the interministerial problems were funneled into them for analysis and resolution. They used to say that 90 per cent of the difficult interministerial problems were always settled at their level because they were fearful if a problem wasn't settled there it might ultimately reach the cabinet. And they were fearful of what the cabinet might do. Therefore, there was a pressure that settled most of the problems at the professional level.

An executive with operating responsibility usually prefers that problems involving his programs be settled at his own level. He fears that consideration at higher levels may inject into the policy-making process judgments that are not soundly based or points of view that are not sufficiently appreciative of the expert opinions of the line operators.

THE STATUS OF BUREAUS

Generally, the similarities in presidential-agency head relationships and agency head-bureau chief relationships are striking. As Herbert Emmerich once said: "If the President is in a constant state of siege, the department heads may be said to be faced with a chronic state of mutiny in their bureaus." While the observation may exaggerate the degree of friction between agency heads and their bureau chiefs, it underlines the vulnerability of departmental controls over bureaus.

Operating Autonomy in the Bureaus. In the competition for operating autonomy, generally bureau chiefs have been more successful in resisting agency-wide controls than their superiors have been in combating presidential integration. Bureau autonomy can be traced to the sprawling patchwork of the executive branch, the weakness of departmental management, the alliance of bureaus with congressional committees and interest groups, and the increasing professional specialization of the civil service. Each of these factors merits further attention.

The unsystematic and untidy collection of 350 bureaus that now constitute the executive branch have been put together haphazardly in bits and pieces. As a famous administrative committee described it, the executive branch grew like a farm—a wing added to the house now, a new barn put up later, a shed built some other time, a silo at one stage, a corn crib at another, until it was spread over the landscape in a thoroughly confusing way. Each bureau or unit has developed its own historical traditions and customary administrative approaches; and each unit gradually developed a vested interest in its statutory powers and political prestige. Created in response to a particular need, each bureau holds firmly to its separatist ways, resisting departmental and presidential leadership.

Weakness of Departmental Management. The drive for bureau autonomy has been strengthened by the traditional weakness of departmental management. Departmental executives cannot match bureau chiefs in experience. From 1933 to 1952, for example, the average tenure of secretaries was 42 months; under secretaries, 23 months; and assistant secretaries, 32 months. During the period 1933-1948, average tenure of bureau chiefs in 70 bureaus was 8½ years. In 1954, in 63 bureaus (not headed by military men or assistant secretaries) in 6 departments, the average length of service of bureau chiefs was just under 5 years, and their average federal experience was 16 years, even though 15 of them were new and had less than 15 months in office at the time.[7] The bureau level of management tends to provide the needed continuity of experience in the government.

In 1955 the Hoover Commission Task Force confirmed the prevailing impression of managerial weakness at departmental levels. It stated:

> The demands upon top management grew so rapidly as Federal functions expanded and international difficulties increased that provision for political executives and management organization to carry this load did not keep pace. The numbers of assistant secretaries, the positions of aides and assistants, and the needed policy staff organizations tended to lag behind requirements.[8]

Under these conditions, as the Commission reported:

> It has . . . been natural that overworked and relatively inexperienced noncareer executives have tended increasingly to rely upon career administrators [in the bureaus] to carry part of the load. While career administrators normally have not been asked to engage directly in political

[7] Data from *Task Force Report on Personnel and Civil Service,* p. 29; and Task Force, "Preliminary Memorandum on Trends in Staffing Political and Administrative Positions," May 3, 1954, p. 8.

[8] *Task Force Report on Personnel and Civil Service,* p. 4.

battle, they have been, over the past number of years, thrust into the defense of agency policies, programs, and activities. It has been common for noncareer executives to make only brief appearances before committees of the Congress and then leave the burden of detailed explanation to career administrators.[9]

The advantage of bureau chiefs and their assistants over departmental executives in experience and political exposure is supplemented significantly by the steady growth of the civil service into a body of relatively permanent professional specialists. Political appointees in departments are usually inexperienced when they assume office and rarely stay long enough to maximize their effectiveness. They are the transient amateurs who are often incapable of exerting firm control over the professional bureaucracy. In this setting, it is not unusual for bureaus to maintain their operating autonomy despite the improved use of central managerial controls of budgeting, program clearance, and personnel administration by departmental staffs.

The Triple Alliance: Bureau, Interest Group, and Congressional Committee. The resistance of bureaus to departmental controls is sustained by their close associations with congressional committees and their interest group constituencies. In fact, a persistent theme in the environment of the federal executive is the development of clusters of power comprising bureaus, congressional committees, and interest groups. As Harvey Mansfield stated, interest groups attempt "to create autonomous and controllable fragments of government, each with a jurisdiction corre-

---

[9] U.S. Commission on Organization of the Executive Branch of the Government, *Personnel and Civil Service,* A Report to the Congress (1955), p. 27.

sponding to the area and scope of the pressure group's interest—autonomous, that is to say, in the sense of independence from the rest of the government, and controllable from the point of view of the pressure group." Their aim is to have a "little government" responsive to and dependent upon them. They strive to develop an island of power consisting of "the pressure group membership which forms the clientele and supports its private government, a separate public agency dedicated to the service of that specific clientele, and a ring of outposts, agents, allies and dependents, reaching into the other centers of power— the White House, the relevant legislative committees and appropriations subcommittees of Congress, the cognate divisions of major executive departments, and the headquarters of the more inclusive pressure groups—that may impinge on its interests."[10] While interest groups are usually frustrated to some degree in achieving their aims, their relative success constitutes a continuing obstacle to departmental integration.

Professional Specialization and Bureau Autonomy. Professional specialization, which has already been referred to, also increases a bureau's resistance to control by those who stand outside it. While the professional qualities of the civil service are a strong force against patronage appointments, they also constitute a force that any political executive must reckon with.

Plentiful evidence of the increasing professionalization of the bureaucracy is at hand. First, since their release from the spoilsmen, government employees have gradually de-

[10] Harvey C. Mansfield, "Political Parties, Patronage, and the Federal Government Service," The American Assembly, *The Federal Government Service: Its Character, Prestige, and Problems* (1954), pp. 106-07.

veloped loyal attachments to the programs of their employing agencies and to their professions. The politics of the spoilsman has been replaced by the politics of program loyalty featuring the employee's dedication to the welfare of his agency. Second, government employees under the protection of the civil service system have evolved an *esprit de corps* based on their group identification. Career systems in the various bureaus are valued and defended because they provide job security and opportunities for promotion and personal development.

A third mark of professional specialization is the establishment of higher standards of performance by various professional groups in federal employment. They try to protect their incumbency and professional status by setting criteria of effective performance that only able people can meet. They assume the self-regulatory task of maintaining professional integrity through codes of ethical conduct. They are not very hospitable to newcomers, especially from outside their professions.

Lastly, professionalization has been promoted by special career systems in several bureaus, such as the Forest Service, the Foreign Service, the commissioned corps in the Public Health Service, and the Federal Bureau of Investigation. In addition, a surprisingly large number of bureaus are staffed by specialized professional personnel of high competence. They include such bureaus as the Census Bureau, the Weather Bureau, the Bureau of Standards, and the Office of Business Economics of the Department of Commerce; the Bureau of Engraving and Printing and the Internal Revenue Service in the Treasury Department; the Geological Survey of the Department of the Interior; the Agricultural Research Service in the Department of Agriculture; the Bureau of Labor Statistics in the

Department of Labor, and others. Moreover, staff officers specializing in budgeting, personnel, economic analysis, and other functions take pride in meeting professional standards that transcend immediate political interests.

While the high standards and professional commitments of the specialized bureaucracies are a major element of strength in the federal government, they may also lead to isolationism by professional groups and become potential obstacles to the policies of political executives. Their strength lies in the bureaus. In the absence of effective central departmental leadership, they become a force for bureau autonomy.

V

The Political Setting: Congress

NEWCOMERS TO WASHINGTON, including government executives, are more bewildered and confused by Congress than by any other part of the political setting. Nothing in private life elsewhere has trained them to understand how Congress operates. Moreover, executives from outside the government commonly come unprepared for political struggle and with slight knowledge of the activities they are expected to direct.

CONGRESSIONAL INFLUENCE IN ADMINISTRATION

In American theory and practice, Congress is equipped with an arsenal of controls that enables it to serve as overseer of the executive branch. Occasionally it is portrayed as a board of directors charged with responsibility to supervise and control the hired managers of federal programs, the President and the heads of executive agencies. While Congress exercises some of the functions of a corporate board of directors, such as control of basic policy and finance, the similarity tends to stop there. The President is not a hired manager but an independently elected representative of the people endowed by the Constitution with specific and general powers. Heads of agencies, moreover, are not represented in Congress, as senior corporate officials are often represented on their boards of directors. In Congress itself, legislative power lies primarily in the hands of more than 100 subcommittees that are rarely held accountable to the House or Senate as a whole. Legislative power is personalized in the hands of committee chairmen and a few ranking members. Internal disunity weakens Congress's capacity to enact affirmative declarations of policy and strengthens its ability to delay, obstruct, and prevent action by the executive branch.

At its enlightened best, Congress uses its power to clarify policy objectives, resolve difficult public questions in ways that satisfy large majorities of the people, highlight serious deficiencies in executive operations, and keep the public informed on issues of public policy. At its worst, Congress weakens the presidency by giving statutory authority directly to bureau chiefs instead of department heads, cuts appropriations designed to strengthen departmental management, specifies administrative procedures minutely, appropriates funds in excessive detail, and plants its appointees in key administrative positions. As long as executive-legislative conflict remains a central feature of American politics, the line that separates constructive from destructive legislative surveillance of the government will remain controversial.

Congress is profoundly influential in the life of a federal executive. Given the lack of unity in Congress and the personalization of legislative power in committee chairmen, it is not surprising that congressional intervention varies considerably from agency to agency and over time. However, in a change of administration and party control, legislative-administrative relations may be particularly troubled:

> . . . men of long experience just change places in the Congress in taking over the important committee posts. The Congress continues to have men of experience in its important positions, and a large pool from which to draw these people, while the executive branch tends to get a group of limited political experience in the highest political positions of secretary, under secretary, and assistant secretary.[1]

Much activity of federal executives involves Congress, but heads of agencies and their principal deputies are outweighed in political experience by the ranking members of congressional committees.

> The contrast in political experience between Members of the Congress and departmental secretaries and assistant secretaries is striking. In the 1st session of the 83rd Cong., at the time that the Eisenhower administration took office, 26 Senators out of a total of 96 had more than 10 years continuous service in the Senate. In the House of Representatives, the percentage of Members of long service is even higher. In the same Congress, 154 Members of the House of Representatives out of a total of 435 had more than 10 years of service in the House. (At the time President Roosevelt took office in 1933, the ratio of Congressmen with long service was even higher. On March 4, 1933, 39 Senators had served 10 or more years and 194 Representatives had served 10 or more years.) Moreover, length of service is even higher among the three highest-ranking members of each party on the legislative committees of

---

[1] U.S. Commission on Organization of the Executive Branch of the Government, *Task Force Report on Personnel and Civil Service* (1955), p. 220.

Congress. In addition to lengthy Congressional service, almost all of the Senators and Representatives who rank
highest on the committees of Congress have substantial
backgrounds of public service in local and State legislative
and executive positions. On the other hand, secretaries,
under secretaries, or assistant secretaries who have significant previous local or State public service are the exceptions rather than the rule.[2]

CONGRESSIONAL INTERVENTION

Variations in congressional intervention from agency to
agency are striking. For example, a former federal executive had quite different experiences as a director of two
bureaus.

OASI and the Employment Service. In the Bureau of
Old Age and Survivors Insurance, the director was subject
to very little influence from Congress as a whole or from
appropriations committees. Only the House Ways and
Means Committee paid much attention to the bureau,
which seldom consulted a committee or member of Congress before taking action. In the United States Employment Service, however, congressional interest ran high.
One House subcommittee regarded the service as its special province, and the service consulted the chairman regularly. "We didn't do much without getting his approval."
The former director recalled:

During World War II, when President Roosevelt issued
executive orders on fair employment practices, we organized the District of Columbia Employment Office. We were
going to make it a single employment office for both whites

[2] *Ibid.*, p. 219, n. 7.

and Negroes. I assumed that this was executive action; as director, I proceeded to take it. We leased building space and fixed the date for opening the office. I was then called before the House committee to review and explain our plans. The chairman wanted to know how the desks were going to be laid out to see whether there was going to be adequate segregation. We did very little without thinking about consulting a congressional committee or a key senator or representative. The chairman in the House took a possessive attitude toward the operation. He wanted us to consult him before we took action, and he expected to pass judgment.

As a non-controversial bureau, OASI operated in a climate of "low temperature" politics. Once the insurance program was enacted by Congress and ruled constitutional by the Supreme Court, the bureau was untroubled by congressional scrutiny. Although it employs about 40 per cent of all employees of the Department of Health, Education, and Welfare, it is financed by one lump-sum appropriation, while the rest of the department is financed by some 60-odd appropriations. Until recently, no special interest group dealt directly with OASI or with congressional committees on matters concerning OASI. In administering the law and interpreting the rights and standing of employees covered by the law, OASI has been granted little discretion. It has been strongly service-oriented in dealing with its millions of customers and has developed perhaps the most efficient data-processing organization in the world.

In contrast, the Employment Service had a powerful organized constituency. As its former director recalled:

I started as director with a naive idea that I ran it, but I discovered that there was a part of the service that no director ran. This was the Veterans Employment Division, which did not even receive its mail in our mailroom. It had a special post office box downtown. When I tried to do something about the division, I learned that it took orders mainly from the Employment Committee of the American Legion. From then on I discussed the work of the division regularly with a committee of the American Legion in Indianapolis.

Forest Service. Since 1905, the Forest Service, located in the Department of Agriculture, has been responsible for promoting the conservation and best use of the nation's forest lands. It conducts a program of forest research, co-operates with states and private owners of forest-lands to stimulate development and proper management of state and private forests, and administers and regulates the public and private use of approximately 150 national forests aggregating over 180 million acres. The service has very little contact with congressmen on its research programs unless the latter want a research unit located in their districts. Although many organizations are interested in the service's co-operative programs, they deal primarily with state officials in pursuit of their demands. Probably less than 20 per cent of the contacts between Congress and the Forest Service relate to the co-operative programs.

Most of the congressional business of the Forest Service deals with the management of national forests. As a knowledgeable observer stated:

The number of congressional calls that the Forest Service gets seems to be related to the number of people affected directly by the service and especially by the number of people who want the service to do something that it is not doing or to stop doing something. In the national forests, for example, the service deals with 800 grazing associations and about 28,000 individual permittees; they all want something from the service in connection with their use of these public lands. These congressional calls have no single source. They come from the agricultural and appropriations committees of both houses and from congressmen representing districts in which national forests are located.

People seem to be going to Congress more and more to transact their business instead of coming directly to the agency. Many congressmen thus become involved in the day-to-day operations of the Forest Service. Sometimes these are matters of small consequence, for example in a recent instance, whether a small office should be moved from one room to another in a local federal building.

Post Office Department. Congressional intervention probably reaches a peak in the Post Office Department. Legislative interest in the department is generated in two ways. First, the department has traditionally been a rich source of political patronage, both in the appointment of postmasters and rural carriers and in the location and construction of post offices. Secondly, the half million employees of the department are tightly organized into powerful unions that have become expert lobbies on Capitol Hill. At times the postal unions achieve such strength that they almost seem capable of dictating to Congress the terms of their employment. Their power is based on numbers and the fact that their members are located in every electoral district of the nation. No other group of federal employees is in such continuing contact with almost every citizen. As a postal executive asserted: "This is the first time I have worked for an employer where the board of directors, in this case Congress, was more sympathetic to labor than to management."

Postal employees, supported by local pride and vigorous congressmen, often resist efforts to reduce the department's deficit by eliminating small post offices that operate at heavy losses. Nor is it a secret that the selection of postmasters and rural carriers is influenced very considerably by members of Congress. On the other hand, congressional participation in the selection of rural carriers has not been grossly harmful. Indeed one departmental executive claimed that:

> We are getting better quality people as rural postmasters and rural carriers than if we had to make the selection ourselves without legislative intervention. We have 38,000 post offices, and more than 30,000 rural carriers. We cannot make as careful an evaluation of candidates for rural positions as members of Congress and their local political committees make. Congressmen learned long ago that it is fatal to recommend a man as rural letter carrier who is incompetent. No one knows more than the people along a rural route just what kind of man serves them. Congressmen dare not recommend someone who is unreliable or in bad repute. The caliber of the men who make up the rural carrier force is higher than that of the city carriers, although there is no legislative interference in the selection of city carriers.[3]

Legislative interference generated by postal unions ranges from matters that concern all postal employees,

[3] The Hoover Commission Task Force on Personnel and Civil Service did not take as charitable a point of view toward the patronage aspects of rural carrier positions. It reported that the Civil Service Commission, which administers examinations for rural carriers, is subject to partisan pressures from congressmen and local political committees "to rerate the papers, to disqualify candidates for technical reasons, or even to void an examination if the politically preferred candidate is not among the first three" from among whom the appointment must be made. *Ibid.*, p. 135.

such as pay increases and fringe benefits, to individual personnel actions in local post offices. According to a departmental executive:

> Congressmen would take little or no interest in many cases, nor would they interfere in matters that appear to be strictly administrative, were it not for the tremendous pressure placed on them very quickly by the employee organizations. To illustrate, the department, after careful study, decided that it could save substantial sums and speed mail service considerably by consolidating mail distribution operations at the Newark post office instead of sharing them between the Newark post office and the terminal at Newark Airport. At that time the department was experimenting with carrying first class mail by air, on a space-available basis. First class mail arriving by train went into the Newark post office. When such mail was carried by air and arrived at the airport, a dispute arose over who should distribute it: postal clerks represented by the National Federation of Post Office Clerks, and the United Association of Post Office Clerks, or the National Postal Transport Association. The department began distribution by the NPTA clerks at the airport terminal. As soon as the department consolidated distribution at the post office, it was deluged with congressional protests. The department was able to convince the House Post Office and Civil Service Committee that consolidation was proper administrative action, but the Senate Post Office and Civil Service Committee forced the department to postpone consolidation three times. The Senate Committee sent its own investigators to Newark to make an investigation. All of this opposition was generated by the NPTA. It was done by alerting local organizations in New Jersey and New York, requesting them to write letters to and make personal calls upon the senators and

congressmen from those states. Postal employee organizations can turn congressional mail on and off in terrific volume within 24 hours, and the number of letters can be formidable.

Undoubtedly the Post Office Department would be able to resist legislative intervention in routine administration more effectively if it had the support and encouragement of an association of postal users with primary concern for improvement in service. While organizations of first-class mailers, second-class mailers, and third-class mailers exist, they are interested primarily in keeping postage rates down. The department cannot aid in organizing an association that might counter the pressures of the postal unions because it is forbidden by law to spend money to influence legislation.

Although the objectives of various organizations of postal employees and users of mail service are different, they are not competitive. In the absence of any conflict of interest among them, the department cannot take advantage of their disunity, nor do the organizations tend to neutralize their influence through division in their ranks. In the Forest Service, however, the recreation interests will often oppose the demands of grazing interests, and the Service has the advantageous support of counter pressure in resisting the demands of a particularly aggressive group. Hence the pressure upon congressmen to intervene in administrative affairs is not as intense or as effective in the Forest Service as it is in the Post Office Department.

Defense Department. Legislative intervention in the administration of defense programs illustrates the impact of personal factors upon congressional scrutiny of administration. An informed executive recalls:

Fifteen to twenty years ago, public works bills enacted by Congress listed and appropriated money for every item separately. Under this system the executive departments were forced to appear before the appropriations committees with a specific plan of what they wanted, item by item. Today the line item budget has given way to bulk appropriations. If executives become careless and fail to justify their budget estimates in detail, the committees will balk. They may decide to approve the budget estimates only on condition that the department concerned clears with the committee before making certain expenditures. Some military units have taken a rather cavalier attitude toward Congress; they thought that they could get money to spend without developing a firm plan. This failure of executives to appreciate the role of Congress in its control of the purse strings has undermined congressional confidence in the agencies and has encouraged congressional intervention in administration.

If federal executives want Congress to grant the appropriations they request and give them administrative latitude afterwards, they have to indicate to Congress that they can be trusted. Also executives have to keep in mind that people on the Hill have problems, too, and sometimes executives can help them by being sympathetic with their problems and by understanding the approaches they take. No executive has to be subservient in order to get along with Congress, but he does need to understand the legislative process and the situations of particular congressmen.

CAUSES OF LEGISLATIVE INTERVENTION

One of the major conclusions of the Round Table was that congressional influence in the life of the federal executive has become more complex, more subtle, and more detailed. Generally, congressional intervention in administration reflects the intensity of friction between the executive and legislative branches. The greater the friction, the more likelihood there is that Congress will interfere in the affairs of the executive branch.

Transacting Business with Congress. Several executives noted the tendency of individuals to transact their administrative business directly with Congress. One commented: "So often the things that come to me through a congressman's office could be settled by our man right there on the ground. Of course, they eventually are referred back to our field offices for settlement. This roundabout method makes more work for me and more business for congressmen to handle."

This tendency can probably be traced in part to rapid expansion of federal functions in recent years and the establishment of hundreds of field offices of federal agencies throughout the country. In many counties, there are thousands of federal employees and dozens of field offices. The individual citizen may be confused by the plethora of federal offices and may not know which one he should deal with on a specific matter. Since his congressman may be the only federal official known to him who is able to deal with all administrative agencies, he turns to him for assistance. A portion of the increase in congressional intervention in administration thus seems to be a reaction to giantism in government. Apparently one way of keeping government personal is to burden congressmen with the role of community broker for the executive branch of government.

Counteracting Presidential Influence. Several factors help to account for variations in congressional behavior toward different agencies at various times. Beginning with the development of the executive budget in 1921 and the creation of the Executive Office of the President in 1939, the role of the presidency as a unifying influence in the executive branch has developed remarkably. While no President has been able to subdue completely the centrifugal forces within the executive branch, recent Presidents have utilized processes of budgeting, personnel management, and administrative reorganization to strengthen their role as federal administrator-in-chief. Congress has reacted to the trend toward executive integration by trying to strengthen its position through salary increases and improved office facilities for members, and more and better staffing for committees. Likewise, increased congressional intervention in administration represents a compensatory effort to counteract the superior resources of the executive branch in collecting and evaluating information, initiating legislative proposals, and interpreting the law.

While legislative intervention in administration antedates the Budget and Accounting Act of 1921, the form and manner of intervention have become more complex. In the words of an astute observer of the legislative process:

> For generations congressmen have felt that, under the separation of powers of our government, they must trust an agent whom they have not appointed with the expenditure of money and the carrying out of important functions. There are a lot of men who are inherently unwilling to give that trust. They are suspicious, and their suspicions are heightened by the manner in which congressional committees are constituted. A man seeks membership on a particular committee usually because his constituency has an interest in the work of that committee, and it is going to profit him politically if he gets on that committee and pro-

tects the interests of his constituents. He is apt to have a strong personal interest in the work of the agencies that fall within the jurisdiction of his committee. His disposition is to delve deeply into the details of administrative operations.

Much congressional intervention arises out of the desire of congressmen to restrain executives and limit their discretion and freedom of action, partly to offset the administrative and political resources of the President and partly to express the legislator's congenital mistrust of executives.

Some General Factors. Congressional intervention tends to be heightened when interest groups that form an organized constituency of an agency are capable of making effective demands upon Congress. An interest group is particularly powerful in securing congressional support provided its aims do not conflict with those of other groups. Conversely, agencies with rival interest group constituents have an opportunity to balance one against another and retain a measure of manipulative power. Occasionally an executive may turn to Congress for support in resisting or overcoming the objectives of organized interests, but he is unlikely to have as much influence in Congress as his group constituency has. Agencies that lack an organized constituency usually operate in a non-controversial area of politics where congressional intervention is apt to be minimal.

The degree of legislative interference in administration is likely to be greater in the case of agencies that exercise considerable administrative discretion than in situations in which administrative latitude is rather narrow. A clear-cut, routine administrative decision based on ample precedent and involving little or no scope for individual judgments normally fails to capture interest or attention on Capitol

Hill. However, both the Post Office Department and the Veterans Administration appear to be major exceptions to the general situation.

Among the committees of Congress, the appropriations committees are likely to be more interested in administrative details than are the substantive standing committees.

Congressmen are usually anxious to use their committee assignments to protect or advance the interests of their districts. As the number of jobs available for patronage appointments has declined, legislators have turned to public works and federal facilities to express their devotion to constituents. The proposed closing of an army camp or a Veterans Administration hospital, the maintenance of a military post exchange that allegedly competes with local retail shops, or the location of a new airport illustrates the issues that invite congressional intervention. Agencies that spend money to construct and maintain conspicuous federal facilities at various places throughout the country are standing targets for congressional intervention, although the possibility of helping a congressman by building a new federal facility or by keeping an existing one in operation may also be instrumental in gaining a larger objective for an agency. Candor compels the admission that the Round Table was unable to determine

> . . . to what extent it is possible to offer a senator an air-field to get the Middle East bill through, or at what point it becomes appropriate for the secretary or his assistant to appoint three nephews of a senator in order to get through an appropriation for a department, or whether it is never appropriate, or whether it helps.

The Personal Equation.   In view of the permissiveness of the legislative process and the importance of personality in Congress, it is not surprising that the personal equation is extremely important in conditioning relations between Congress and an agency. The character and personality of a committee chairman may be crucial. Some subcommittee chairmen develop a paternalistic and provincial attitude toward certain agencies. In such cases, it may be sound practice for executives to cultivate the trust and confidence of the chairmen in order to turn the personal relationship to the advantage of the executive branch. In some instances executives may have no effective choice; the tradition of close congressional control may be so powerful that a new executive can only follow his predecessor in beating the well-worn path to the door of his committee chairman. In a few instances, a chairman may be able to maintain full control over a frustrated committee through the force of his personality. All negotiations with certain agencies tend to be handled by that chairman, usually to the advantage of the agencies. But if the chairmanship should change, committee members may attempt to limit the authority of the new chairman with consequences that may be upsetting to the agency.

The degree of congressional intervention may also depend to some extent on the appraisal that key members of Congress make of an executive. By his approach and attitude toward Congress and its members, an executive influences his congressional relations. Executives who become sophisticated specialists in the administration of particular governmental programs and aim toward the development of a tidy, rational organization may find it difficult to face elected officials who are necessarily concerned more with political achievement than the requisites of efficient management. The lack of executive understanding of the congressional environment is probably more destructive of sound executive-legislative relations than any other single factor.

One of the more common sources of difficulty is the lack of recognition by executives of the role of Congress in legislation. As one expert on the legislative process stated:

> Some executives go too far in developing a pre-cooked piece of legislative material that is handed to Congress in expectation that it will be enacted substantially as submitted. Most legislators accept their limitations as initiators of legislative proposals, but they will not rubber-stamp a bill. They want to be consulted in advance, and they insist upon having a real opportunity to modify the proposals of the executive branch. Executives who ignore the sensitivity of Congress in this area often goad congressmen into taking "remedial" action involving subtle and complex methods designed to make the administration subservient. If the executive branch dealt with Congress more rationally on legislative proposals, there would probably be less application of these "remedial" measures and therefore less interference in administrative affairs.

Advance consultation with members of Congress on proposed legislation is only a special instance of the process of communication between the two branches. Most executives believe that congressmen are more likely to be even-handed in their actions affecting administrative agencies when they understand the agency and what it is trying to do. "When they don't understand it, you are in trouble," one executive said. "If you don't communicate, you get these artificial barriers put on you. The more contact I have with members of Congress, the less difficulties I seem to have."

Often an executive with little or no previous participation in political affairs seems unprepared to make the accommodations and compromises that are the hallmark of the American legislative process. The executive with many years of experience in the civil service and much greater exposure to the political environment, however, is usually prepared to make a substantially greater effort to adjust to the realities of congressional behavior. Bureau chiefs, congressmen, and leaders of key interest groups have been in Washington a long time. They know each other and how to get along with one another. On the other hand, as one participant observed: "The strangers in town are the President and the President's men."

TRENDS IN RELATIONS WITH CONGRESS

The Round Table discussed recent trends in legislative-executive relations in three areas: the staffing of legislative committees, the increasing use of legislative veto devices, and legislative liaison staffs in the administrative agencies.

Legislative Staffing. The staffs of legislative committees form a significant part of the legislative environment for the executive. As a result of the Legislative Reorganization Act of 1946, stronger and larger staffs have emerged in most legislative committees, some of which have become influential forces in dealing with executive agencies.

The status of legislative staffs varies considerably from committee to committee and over time. When a chairman is not an informed student of the businesss of his committee or is not a particularly forceful person, his staff director can become a dominant force. The staff director may be able to wield the influence of the committee in dealing with executive agencies and make demands upon the executive branch in the chairman's name. On the other hand, a few chairmen of long tenure may emerge as the best informed and most knowledgeable men in Washington in certain areas of public affairs. Their personal competence and political power may be so great that they need not depend on their staffs for information, detailed analyses, or liaison with particular executives. In such instances, the committee's power is personalized, and the status of the committee staff tends to be insignificant.

Since 1946, a tradition of continuing tenure has developed on committee staffs despite changes in party control. Continuity in staffing has been especially helpful to executives in those occasional instances when a large turnover in committee membership has occurred. An informed staff can supply much of the knowledge and understanding that new committee members may lack. Staff continuity has also produced an apparent evenness in the approach of committees to legislative problems and a degree of sophistication about committee business that did not exist previously. On the other hand, the development of a quasi-permanent bureaucracy serving the legislative branch has stimulated legislative interest in the details of administrative operations and occasionally has enabled committees to delve deeply into matters that federal executives consider to be administrative prerogatives.

In certain cases committee staffs may be unimportant or superfluous and in others quite helpful to executives. For example, an executive of the Defense Department stated:

> The chairmen of committees are the point of contact for us in Congress. We rarely deal with the staff members of either the Armed Services Committee or the appropriations subcommittee in the House. And as far as Congress is concerned, these two committees are the hub around which the Defense Department operates. They provide the money and judge the program. Both chairmen are highly regarded

and very expert in military affairs. With different chairmen, our position with Congress may change considerably.

Executives may discover that close contacts with legislative staffs may develop a line of indirect communication with committee members when more direct contact has failed. On the other hand, they may endeavor to work closely with committee members in order to resist an aggressive staff. One executive noted:

> Our experience has been that we have had to develop a direct relationship with committee members as an offset to some of the pet objectives of the professional staff. We were working on a rather technical problem, and there was some tendency for committee members to defer on technical points to the professional judgment of the staff.

Continuity in legislative staffing has brought about a close relationship between committee staffs and career executives. Sometimes the career staffs of the two branches maintain contacts without specific participation by members of committees or by the politically appointed executives in the agencies. These relations gradually develop into meaningful bonds; they provide a line of communication that often has a marked bearing on the environment of the executive. The bonds between the two career staffs may be particularly strong where interchanges of personnel occurred. For example, one executive reported that "in the atomic energy field, there were shifts of personnel from the Joint Committee on Atomic Energy in Congress to the Atomic Energy Commission and vice versa. Sometimes it was not entirely clear where some of the sources of direction were actually located." Similar interchanges of staff have occurred between the Joint Committee on Taxation and the Treasury Department.

Does the legislative bureaucracy rival the executive bureaucracy? Or does it collaborate with it? Do the two staffs form a collaborative bureaucracy in which decisions are worked out co-operatively by the committee staffs and career officials in the agencies while congressmen and politically appointed executives tend to be cut out of the stream of decision making? How do the relationships between the two bureaucracies, whether rival or collaborative, affect the influence of the politically appointed executive? The Round Table was unable to give firm answers to these questions. Rather the diversity of experience was emphasized. One executive summarized the Round Table's views:

> I think there is a play of both rivalry and collaboration. You can't generalize. I have seen it work both ways. Moreover, it will work differently over time and in different segments of the government. The personal equation explains some of the diversity. A rivalry situation can be converted into a collaborative one through personality adjustments of one kind or another.

Another executive was more willing to generalize:

> I think you could say that there is rivalry between the political executive and the legislative bureaucrat and collaboration between the career executives and the legislative staff member, not exclusively, but it would tend to be that way. The tendency would be to have more of the elements that create rivalry between the political executive and the committee staff man than there would be between the career men on Capitol Hill and the career men at the other end of Pennsylvania Avenue. The continuity of committee staff that we have had among the better staffs in the past

ten or twelve years has forced both rivalry and collaboration to an extent that we did not have twenty years ago.

Congress tends to regard some agencies as being subject to more than the usual amount of legislative surveillance. These "legislative" agencies, like the independent regulatory commissions, usually experience more rivalry than collaboration in their dealings with committee staffs. Congress also has traditionally treated certain areas of public policy as peculiarly its own province. For instance, in the past most legislation affecting the postal service was initiated by the House Post Office and Civil Service Committee. The Committee and its staff operated on the assumption that the postal service was primarily the business of Congress rather than the Postmaster General and the President. Executive-legislative relations normally were not collaborative.

The Legislative Veto.   In addition to action by individual members of Congress and by committees and their staffs, Congress as a whole can intervene in the affairs of the executive branch. Since the decline in the enactment of highly detailed appropriations and specific spending limitations, Congress has sought other devices to maintain detailed control over administrative operations. One device is the legislative veto, which has become a source of increasing concern to the executive branch. Since the passage of the Reorganization Act of 1939, when the President accepted a provision for legislative veto of reorganization proposals in order to get the measure approved, Congress has demonstrated considerable ingenuity in devising various forms of the legislative veto. One expert stated:

The legislative veto includes telling an executive department by statute that it can do something only after it gets the affirmative consent of a congressional committee or a series of committees; or that it can do something only so long as Congress does not forbid the action by concurrent resolution, which the President never gets a chance to veto; or that either house of Congress can stop executive action with or without a constitutional majority of that house.

A second executive traced the development of formal legislative controls partly to improvement in executive personnel.

As a group, federal executives are more ingenious and more sophisticated than they were twenty years ago. Many of them now assert their independence of Congress to a degree that did not used to be dreamed of. So Congress finds it expedient to make wider use of the legislative veto to intrude on the affairs of the executive branch.

The use of veto devices is undoubtedly affected by special considerations. The independence of regulatory commissions, like the Federal Trade Commission, consists principally in their location outside of an executive department, which is presumably accompanied by some protection against presidential influence. Congress is fond of describing the commissions as "arms of the Congress." One congressional technique to "insulate" the commissions from presidential control is to subject reorganization proposals to a legislative veto. In this manner, in 1950 the President was prevented from designating the chairman of the Interstate Commerce Commission.

Use of the legislative veto may be stimulated by poor

executive performance, especially in preparing and justifying budget estimates. As one executive recalled:

> Some years ago, most appropriations carried a number of limitations controlling the expenditure of funds. In the Department of the Army appropriation there were about 140 limitations, and the Navy had about the same number. By 1958, all administrative limitations in the budgets of the three military departments had disappeared, and the number of individual appropriations had been reduced drastically. As Congress has moved further away from a line-item budget, it is sensitive to incompetent budget making and may accept some veto device as an expression of its lack of confidence in a particular department. This is what it has done in the case of some military activities, and it takes the department concerned a long time to rid itself of such controls.

One of the participants was deeply concerned about the growing use of the legislative veto during the Truman and Eisenhower administrations:

> Congress has gone far in recent years in adopting this device to intrude on the affairs of the executive branch. While a legislative veto arrangement may be quite acceptable to the individual administrator from the point of view of the constitutional theory of separation of powers, it represents an actually or potentially dangerous intrusion upon the prerogatives of the President to see that the laws are faithfully executed. The most serious aspect of these devices is the requirement that an agency official come into agreement with a House committee and a Senate committee as a prerequisite to lawful action. This procedure of "coming-into-agreement" certainly dilutes the constitutional role

of the President as general manager of the executive branch.

Legislative Liaison Staffs.   In recent years, most large agencies have maintained offices specializing in congressional relations. A few departments have assistant secretaries for congressional relations, but most agencies have lower ranking officers. What impact has the legislative liaison function had on the congressional environment of executives? Once again, experience varies from agency to agency; however, most of the executives who participated in the Round Table were impressed more with the liabilities than the benefits flowing from the work of legislative liaison staffs. Several participants observed that these staffs tend to produce more legislative proposals than executives can advocate in any given congressional session, and seldom take many burdens of legislative communication off the shoulders of executives. However, another executive cautioned:

> Before you abolish these liaison jobs, you have to take into account that these staffs are often valuable as a buffer for the executive, especially if he is in conflict with a particular congressman or senator. If so, you can turn to the liaison man for help in smoothing matters over and getting some information. They have been pretty helpful to me at times. They have paved the way for various things. Most of them are closely associated with congressional people and others with political influence, and they can often accomplish something that other executives cannot.

Different views were expressed by other executives. One stated:

> The liaison staffs are useful in providing a consistent channel for the processing of legislative documents. They

provide a useful mechanical apparatus, but if the department has a draft bill that it really needs, they do not help to sell it, they do not understand it, and they do not have to live with it. The executive in charge of the matters involved in the proposed legislation has to carry the ball in Congress. He is the only one who knows enough to be effective with Congress.

A second observed:

We have a liaison man who channels back to me from members of Congress requests to promote this fellow, appoint that one, move an office, and so on. Many of these things might never come to us if our liaison man did not spend a lot of time on Capitol Hill, running into administrative assistants to congressmen. These fellows probably are useful in letting us know how a legislative proposal stands at a particular time, but not in helping to get the bill passed.

The majority of the participants agreed with the observation that the attention given by executives to the legislative function has grown, but that unfortunately there is now less selectivity on the part of the executives in deciding what legislative measures are important enough to be given a high priority. "The legislative programs of federal agencies have tended to grow almost in direct proportion to the number of people concerned with the legislative process. To the extent that it focuses attention on matters requiring action it is beneficial, but it unfortunately induces a secretary to carry too many legislative proposals to Congress, with the result that the committees have a very hard time choosing among the available alternatives. Committee members sometimes feel that they are being overwhelmed with a mass of legislative proposals."

Two or three members, upon reflection, thought that a better case might be made for the liaison process.

We have been pretty rough on the formal process of legislative liaison. Some legislative representatives have done a pretty good job. The only ones you hear about are those that fail. You never hear about the ones who have been awfully useful to their department and who go on quietly month after month getting the department's view before a congressional committee.

One member added: "Even if the experience thus far has not been generally good, I would not dare take on the job of being head of an agency without one. Maybe most of the jobs are not well-filled now, but they don't have to be so."

On balance, this legislative liaison activity appears to be useful in providing a systematic procedure for channeling legislative requests, although some executives find that it tends to overburden them with legislative business and is not sufficiently selective in determining what legislative proposals are given top priority. These positions may be filled with inherently inadequate personnel so long as they are regarded as especially suitable for patronage appointments. Truly skillful legislative representatives who aggressively represent their departments would probably prove to be very valuable assistants to cabinet members and agency heads.

THE PROBLEM OF COMPROMISE

Communication between members of Congress and executives is conditioned by differences in the approach and methods of the two groups. Members of Congress generally prefer direct informal contacts with executives and become formal when informality proves unsatisfactory to them. Executives, on the other hand, tend to be more institutional-minded and formal than their legislative overseers.

The congressional approach is often personal and motivated by special concerns for constituent or sectional interests, while executives usually strive to develop a comprehensive view of the public interest in their specialized areas. On the other hand, congressmen tend to be generally aware of public desires and preferences and have some responsibility for placing executive proposals in a broad context of public policy. The men on Capitol Hill usually are expert in the political art of compromise, while the executive is skilled in the managerial art of rational decision making.

Congress expects executives to assume the initiative in establishing congressional relations, and it generally prefers close contacts with bureaus to relations with presidential representatives. In recent years the executive branch has relied extensively on interdepartmental committees, special cabinet committees, and advisory committees for the development of public policy proposals in controversial or complex areas. Often the reports of such committees have become the basis of fully developed presidential proposals to Congress. These reports have usually defined the terms and conditions of the arguments made by the executive branch in support of its recommendations.

In such instances, the head of a department or agency, who carries the main responsibility for advocating the administration's legislative proposals, is already committed in detail as well as in principle when he appears before a congressional committee. The executive is so committed to a previously agreed course of action that he has little room for negotiation. Congress, however, insists on compromise. If the administration is unprepared to compromise, it may lose more than necessary in the legislative process, and the presidency itself may lose in stature.

The tendency for executives to appear before Congress in defense of a position that has been worked out comprehensively within the administration without consultation with congressional committees has caused some deterioration in executive-legislative communications. Congress does not like to be confronted with a case that has been developed on the basis of special committee reports. Such reports inject persons into the relationship between congressmen and executives who, from the congressional viewpoint, are not normally involved in the regular flow of business between departments and congressional committees. Congress prefers face-to-face dealings with departmental representatives. It resents insufficient recognition by the executive branch of the congressional interest in legislation.

The Round Table concluded that legislative positions taken by the executive branch, whether developed at the departmental level or by some more elaborate mechanism of interdepartmental co-ordination, should never lack a substantial bargaining element. When executives become overcommitted in defense of legislative proposals, they can negotiate with Congress only within narrow limits, the compromise process is stymied, Congress balks, and the President's program suffers.

The reliance by the Eisenhower administration on these co-ordinating devices can probably be explained by the desirè of Republican executives, who had been out of power for a long period, to think things through for themselves before submitting legislative proposals to Congress. Another contributing factor may have been the administration's desire to improve the formal organization of the executive branch by adapting the concept of the military general staff to civilian administration.

VI

The Political Setting:
Parties and Interest Groups

THE TENDENCY OF FEDERAL executives to view political parties skeptically stems undoubtedly from the divisive nature of American parties. Some of that tendency, however, is the result of the public assault upon the political party as an institution, which began more than 75 years ago in the civil service reform movement. As parties have declined as sources of executive personnel, their impact upon the environment of federal executives has become blurred and confused.

A LOOK AT POLITICAL PARTIES

Parties generally have not been helpful in charting alternative courses of action or in identifying the public interest in specific areas of public policy. Executives cannot rely on party rivalry to illuminate dark corners of public policy. An executive with many years of federal experience observed:

> The party apparatus as such does not debate the issues in ways that clarify the problems facing the executives. The trouble is that there is no consolidated party position on most issues. You can appear before a congressional committee today on almost any issue without being able to tell

which party is which. They do not divide clearly by party, and the voting alliances supporting you in Congress shift with each issue.

Although the impact of the party system on executives is cloudy, two trends may be noted. When the party becomes involved in executive affairs, it tends to concern itself with specific matters at a relatively low level in the administrative hierarchy. Secondly:

> When the party or a faction of a party intervenes in administration, it usually does so at the behest of an interest group rather than in defense of the public interest. That is a broad generalization, but it is frequently valid. When some part of the party apparatus moves to influence the executive branch, it is usually helping a particular interest group that has a powerful voice within that party.

Patronage.   Patronage was not invented by the United States, nor is it peculiar to government. Nevertheless, in the past it has played a significant role in American politics. Half a century ago, when machine politics were under attack by progressive reformers, a Tammany philosopher made the classic argument for political patronage:

> First, this great and glorious country was built up by political parties; second, parties don't hold together if their workers don't get the offices when they win; third, if the parties go to pieces, the government they built must go to pieces, too; fourth, then there'll be h--l to pay.[1]

Formerly, a political party needed patronage for three purposes: to build and sustain an organization of professional party workers, to attract blocs of voters, and to minimize factional divisions within party ranks or create division within the ranks of the opposing party. Today the

[1] William L. Riordan, *Plunkitt of Tammany Hall* (1948), p. 18.

majority party continues to demand patronage to reward faithful and effective service, and government executives still need the support of the party in order to govern. But profound changes in the party system have accompanied a sharp decline in patronage. Ethical standards in party and government are probably higher today than at the turn of the century, and crude opportunities to profit from political action have undoubtedly shrunk. The party is no longer the agent of charity and welfare to teeming immigrant populations. It must meet the test of public scrutiny before TV cameras, national magazines, and metropolitan newspapers. And it must counter increasingly vigorous competition from trade associations and interest groups whose stock-in-trade is the satisfaction of group wants.

Since the enactment of the Pendleton Act in 1883, which created an embryo civil service system in the executive branch of the national government, most Presidents have exerted influence to extend the merit system and to limit patronage. They discovered that the power of appointment does not often help a President to maintain control of his party and may encourage others to convert it to their own uses. Senators and representatives seek to use patronage to advance their interests in their home constituencies and to strengthen their influence in executive agencies. And interest groups seek to place their candidates in agencies central to their economic interests. Patronage, therefore, seems to be a force that leads to further diffusion of leadership and responsibility in the executive branch and constitutes a potential, if not actual, threat to the President.

If patronage is on the decline, it is not extinct. It appears to be more important for positions in field offices than for those in Washington. It tends to be more significant for new functions, especially controversial ones, where the need for political support is critical. Because the President needs the most competent and loyal men he can find for his cabinet and for staff positions in the White House offices, the major positions available to the parties for patronage purposes, outside of a few key ambassadorships, are likely to be those that fall between the department head and his bureau chiefs—under and assistant secretaries, executive assistants, legal and policy advisers, and the like, and those that are filled in field offices.

Parties as Sources of Executive Talent.   One of the striking characteristics of American parties is the ineptness of party machinery in providing able candidates for executive positions who will be loyal to the administration in office. The patronage system cannot supply usable candidates in substantial numbers because of the lack of cohesion within the parties. National party committees are anchored in the state and local parties rather than in the presidential wing of the parties. Furthermore, in either party the congressional party machinery tends to be more right-wing in politics than the presidential wing of the party.

The split between the presidential and nonpresidential wings of the party in office varies from party to party and from time to time. It tends to be widest when the President has not risen through the party ranks, and the wider the split, the less likely is the party apparatus to supply satisfactory candidates for executive positions. Both Presidents Roosevelt and Truman participated actively in the Democratic party throughout their careers and used the party machinery more than President Eisenhower has.

When Roosevelt went to Warm Springs, there would be a group of southern politicians three blocks long waiting to get in to talk with him, from ward heelers up to state chairmen and state committeemen. When Eisenhower goes anywhere, there is a line of business men half a block long waiting to see him along with military and government people. Without praising or reproaching either one, I think that Presidents who came up through the party apparatus were much more at home in dealing with politicians. They had a more philosophic view of the role of the politician, had better control of the party machinery, and were more likely to use it. A President to whom politics has been a career usually finds politicians more congenial than persons in other professions. If President Eisenhower is succeeded by such a nominee, we will probably witness a resurgence of the party in staffing the federal government.

Other factors contribute to the weakness of parties as suppliers of executive talent. A personnel expert noted that:

> Those who run the party machinery for the most part have little understanding of the executive function and the qualities that are necessary in order to make the executive branch function effectively, and the people who tend to cluster around the party offices are only infrequently those who may make an effective contribution.

Parties have no mechanism for screening and recommending suitable candidates and no standards for judging executive competence. They might be able to develop satisfactory standards and procedures if they become more unified, but they are not able to do so in their present condition. The parties have never achieved a high degree of effectiveness in administering their own activities. As one student of parties stated:

> The task of running a successful political campaign is a big organizing job that requires a lot of executive talent. But to a considerable extent the job is not done well. If either party did a really first-class job of administering its own affairs, it would be in a far better position to supply able candidates for executive positions.

Defeated congressmen, who are the candidates most readily available to the party apparatus, are often weak in executive ability. Consequently the movement of former legislators into the executive branch has been infrequent. Finally, general economic conditions affect the processes of political patronage. In a full-employment economy, the pressure for political appointment at high levels is very slight.

Pessimistic attitudes of executives toward parties originate partly in the capacity of the party in opposition to maintain a barrage of criticism directed at executive agencies. An executive without previous experience finds it difficult to adjust to an environment in which his program is under constant attack. A former executive stated:

> Party criticism can be brutal to an executive. Somebody in the opposing party may have been assigned to see that the public is made fully aware of everything that is inept in the agency. He would point out the ineptness continuously, and the executive has to learn to live with his aggressive critics.

Another executive added:

> If the executive has come up through the political ranks, he is probably accustomed to this political crossfire. It is the

breath of life for him. But the career executive in geology, medicine, agronomy, or whatever field it is, finds this party criticism onerous. If through forbearance or dedication, he stays in federal service and eventually becomes an executive, he finds himself frustrated again and again because he cannot recruit competent professional persons who are willing to subject themselves to this constant bird-dogging that may have no relation to actual performance. Even with pay equivalent to salaries in industry, many competent professionals will not come into government because they refuse to subject themselves to such criticism. The party system certainly makes the task of recruiting professional talent more difficult.

The significance of political parties in the life of a federal executive depends largely on the character and training of the President, his relations to the party apparatus, general economic conditions, and the situation of the parties themselves. If political parties become more cohesive and party machinery more centralized, they might conceivably affect the executive's environment more directly and even beneficially. At the moment, however, parties are probably less significant than interest groups in the executive's environment.

THE INFLUENCE OF INTEREST GROUPS

Organized interest groups constitute a very important aspect of the environment of the executive in government. They subject him to pressure to confer special privileges and to discriminate in their favor. They may be capable of manufacturing or exploiting storms of criticism that keep the political atmosphere turbulent. On the other hand, through their political support, they may smooth an executive's political path to Congress and strive to protect him from attack by other executives and agencies and rival interest groups. The diffusion of formal political controls in the national government serves to magnify the influence of organized private groups in public affairs, and in varying degrees, the executive agencies have come to rely on them for knowledge, information, and political support.

A major aim of the interest groups is to induce Congress to create agencies in their own image to the greatest degree possible. They aim to have established in the government autonomous organizations whose jurisdictions correspond to the interest of the pressure groups. They endeavor to make it possible for these agencies to remain relatively independent of the executive branch as a whole and therefore subject more readily to their influence.

> Viewing government as an instrument, the aim of a pressure group . . . is to have a "little government" beholden to it for its existence and powers, responsive to its policy dictates, endowed with sufficient legal authority and funds to carry through its programs, and able politically to ward off or disregard the impulses and restraints that come from the co-ordinating centers and mechanisms of the larger government as a whole.[2]

Interest groups try to influence the appointment of persons sympathetically disposed toward their aims and values. In addition they attempt to force agencies to negotiate continuously with them and to grant them membership on advisory committees that keep them fully informed

[2] Harvey C. Mansfield, "Political Parties, Patronage, and the Federal Government Service," The American Assembly, *The Federal Government Service: Its Character, Prestige, and Problems* (1954), pp. 106-07.

of operational details. Often such groups as business, labor, professions, Indians, veterans, and farmers secure official representation within an agency and these representatives look to their own groups for guidance rather than to the executives who head their agencies.

Interest Groups as Constituencies. The centrifugal tendencies of American political arrangements encourage the organization of interest groups to influence government activities. Every agency tends to have a constituency in roughly the same way that a senator or representative has, except that it is likely to be defined not in terms of congressional districts or states but rather in terms of functionally-oriented groups that are nation-wide or regional in scope.

The federal executive must negotiate more or less continuously with organized interests concerned with his programs. He must live not merely with the presidency, congressmen, party leaders, executive colleagues, and subordinate administrative officials, but also with the leaders of interest groups. Agencies whose programs are deeply concerned with affairs of business enterprise tend to become dependent upon their organized clientele for detailed technical knowledge and information, while those that also regulate private businesses and industrial practices must win the consent of their regulated clientele in order to be effective.

The problems that an executive faces as he confronts his organized constituency vary from agency to agency. Some agencies, like the Departments of Agriculture, Labor, and Commerce, were created at the behest of farmers, workers, and businessmen respectively and have evolved a tradition of close identification with those interests. Other agencies lying outside the mainstream of executive departments, like the independent regulatory commissions, have jurisdiction over a single industry or group of related industries with whom they develop extremely close relations and upon whose support their survival comes to depend. Generally the free co-operation of an agency with its regulated clientele tends to be compatible with the public welfare only when the executives of the agency are guided by a well-defined, accepted public policy.

Relations between executives and interest groups are also influenced considerably by the attitude of the President toward the agency and by the conditions that limit his power of appointment. In making selections of cabinet officers, the President must be guided to some extent by the felt need to represent a variety of interests in cabinet and other executive appointments. Geography, religious observance, position in the party, and economic status are among the factors that the President may find it necessary to consider. Occasionally, especially in a noncabinet agency, an interest group may influence directly the appointment of an executive, who may be periodically reminded of the origin of his appointment.

Monolithic and Competitive Constituencies.   The executive's relationship to interest groups is influenced directly by the kind of constituency that confronts his agency. A monolithic constituency, like the one that deals with the Veterans Administration, has much more influence than a competitive constituency composed of several groups with conflicting objectives, but monolithic constituencies are rather rare in the federal government. The Departments of Agriculture, Labor, and Commerce have had secretaries who regarded themselves as mouthpieces of particular groups, but the groups have become more numerous and less single-minded. In Agriculture, for example, there is considerable competition now between various farm groups on both a regional and a commodity basis. A secretary can improve his capacity to resist the influence of organized farmers by playing one group against another and retain a measure of maneuverability that would be lacking if the agricultural constituency was wholly united in its aims. Executives who deal with pluralistic interests can usually exercise more leadership and initiative than those dealing with a single, unified pressure group.

Continuing and Transient Groups. Some interest groups have a continuing, sustained existence, while others are transient or momentary. Groups with direct, tangible interests in governmental programs are likely to be more or less permanent with salaried staffs and Washington representatives. Transient groups, on the other hand, tend to be based primarily on sentiment or emotion. The latter are diffuse, but they are usually ripe for demagogic leadership and sometimes can be mobilized quickly in response to a momentary crisis.

While everyone is interested in health, and good health is also good politics, the federal health agencies have to deal with highly organized constituencies representing the medical profession in general and in specialized areas, such as cancer, heart disease, muscular dystrophy, or mental health. These groups are affected directly and tangibly by the activities of federal health agencies and they maintain organizations that remain in intimate contact with those agencies. One executive commented:

The health field has become highly organized in the last

decade. Health affects all of us, our wives, mothers-in-law, friends. Groups are active in one area of health after another. They shift their interests depending on which disease is in the limelight and which in their opinion requires more funds for research. They remain identified and concerned generically with health. Now an executive can ride out the storm created by a transient pressure group, but he won't be able to do that if the pressures hit him day in and day out, year after year. And I don't think any executive really ever gets hardened to it.

The Bureau of Narcotics in the Department of the Treasury is an example of an agency with a diffuse, transient constituency. The Bureau is responsible for administering and enforcing federal laws that regulate the use, sale, and transportation of narcotics. While nearly everyone is opposed to drug addiction, the nature of the public interest in narcotics control is not clear. No pressure group comparable to those active in mental health or heart disease concerns itself with problems of narcotics, but the emotion that has been created in opposition to drug addiction constitutes a moral influence that can be aroused from time to time. The anti-narcotics constituency is disorganized and transient, but: "It has the ability to be crystallized in the snap of a finger, with the result that the congressional committees may want to give the Bureau funds sufficient to employ an additional one hundred enforcement officers which the Bureau may not be able to use effectively."

Selective Pressures.   A federal executive must be prepared to deal with selective strategic pressures as well as mass pressures generated by huge organizations like the postal unions or the American Legion. Often a small group of informed, well-known persons with influential political contacts can exert more influence than a mass organization with thousands of members. As one participant stated:

> The Veterans Administration is in touch with a great faceless mass of veterans, but there is another kind of pressure group that may, in certain circumstances, be more effective: the small group of informed individuals who are not professional lobbyists but who have effective contacts in the executive branch, in the President's office, in the Bureau of the Budget, and among the significant members of certain congressional committees. One or two dozen of them can do more in a few quiet talks than 100,000 telegrams. They can sometimes do more in a day than the other can do in months.

Another executive recalled the occasion when Dr. Paul Dudley White, the heart specialist who treated President Eisenhower, was asked by a congressional committee to testify at a hearing on the Public Health Service: "The committee organized a whole set of hearings around Dr. White. Everybody else had to conform to his convenience. His testimony took a whole morning, and it had more effect on the committee than testimony from a thousand members of the general public might have had.

Resisting and Using Interest Groups. The capacity of administrative agencies to maintain some freedom of action in the face of strong constituent pressures varies a great deal. So-called old-line agencies have usually been considered to be inappropriate agencies for administration of a new program during an emergency because their initiative in tackling new tasks would be minimized by well-established clientele relations. During World War II and the Korean war, new agencies unhampered by established constituencies were created to deal with problems of mobilizing the civilian economy for war and defense. Recent experience suggests that the creation of new agencies may be an effective method to circumvent established constituent pressures.

Interest groups can be important sources of support to government agencies, and federal executives need to mobilize them for constructive assistance. One career executive offered the generalization that "a federal executive, especially a career man who expects to continue in his post for some time, must become interested and active in organizations that have a professional interest in his programs." He added: "The smart executive must be active in organizations outside of government in order to be able to mobilize their support when he needs it. If he can organize effective counter pressure, he can maintain the integrity of his program despite the pressures seeking to influence his behavior."

As one former executive pointed out, the character and talents of an executive have a marked bearing on the degree of influence which can be exerted upon him by pressure groups:

> In my experience the administrative activities most exposed to interest group influence are those in which the executive lacks the ability or the courage to reconcile special interests with the public interest before committees of Congress, the press, or any other area of public opinion. If the top executive is unwilling to stand up to private interests, you cannot expect the organization to be anything but vulnerable to those pressures. It is the man who leads the activity that counts in this situation. It requires more than character and good intentions. The executive must have the ability to debate, to bargain, and to negotiate.

Several executives agreed that:

> It is the duty of the federal executive not to be so sub-
> servient to a constituency that he is afraid to stand up to
> interest groups served by his agency. A notable example of
> outstanding courage in dealing with pressure groups was
> General Omar Bradley when serving as head of the Vet-
> erans Administration. General Bradley was the only ad-
> ministrator of veterans' affairs, out of four or five in the
> past thirty years, who was willing to take a public position
> on a policy matter which differed from the position of the
> veterans' organizations. General Bradley was chastised for
> doing so, he alienated the veterans' groups, and he prob-
> ably lost the support of those groups for the recommenda-
> tions which were made by the commission he later headed
> to study veterans' benefits. But before he left the Veterans
> Administration, he made certain recommendations to Con-
> gress in the closing days of a session, and eleven days from
> the time he made the recommendations, the bill was on
> the President's desk for signature—a bill which probably
> saved the taxpayers as much as a billion dollars, and per-
> haps more.

Efforts to Regulate Interest Groups. In 1946 Congress
undertook for the first time to control interest groups in the
Federal Regulation of Lobbying Act. The law actually involves very little regulation. Any person or organization
soliciting or receiving money to be used "principally to
aid", "or the principal purpose" of which person or organization is to aid the passage or defeat of legislation before
Congress is required to register with the Clerk of the
House of Representatives and to file quarterly reports
showing all moneys actually received and expended, including the names and addresses of all persons contributing $500 or more, or to whom $10 or more has been paid.

Each lobbyist must disclose "the name and address of the person by whom he is employed, and in whose interest he appears or works, the duration of such employment, how much he is paid and is to receive, by whom he is paid or is to be paid, how much he is paid for expenses, and what expenses are to be included." The required data must be published at quarterly intervals in the *Congressional Record*. Penalties for those convicted under the act range up to a $10,000 fine and a five-year prison term and a three-year ban against further lobbying.

The language of the statute is vague and confusing, and it has encouraged a good deal of noncompliance. No enforcement agency is provided, and the pattern of lobbying does not appear to have been affected by the law. Several organizations have refused to register on the ground that they are not lobbies as defined by the act. In any case, the information filed is scanty and gives little indication of the significance of a lobbyist's political activity.

Even though the act provides for only a weak measure of lobby control, serious constitutional doubts have been raised against it. The three-year ban against further lobbying has been attacked as depriving a person of his basic right of petition under the First Amendment. Others have charged that the act fails to provide an ascertainable standard of guilt and therefore violates the requirement of due process of law. Finally in 1954, the Supreme Court held by a 5-3 vote in United States v. Harriss (347 U.S. 612) that the act was constitutional but applied only to lobbyists who enter into direct communication with members of Congress with respect to pending or proposed legislation and does not extend to those who seek to influence legislation indirectly by working through public opinion.

Special interests, like the decentralized party system and the divisive organization of individual and committee power in Congress, generally are not congenial to the unity and rationality that executives strive to achieve. But they do create opportunities and challenges for the executive who is willing to face them courageously.

VII

Getting and Keeping
Able Executives in Government

IN AN ARTICLE HEADLINED " 'Help Wanted' Sign Out . . . Government Gets Few Takers," a weekly magazine reported in 1957 that business executives, formerly willing to take important executive posts in the Eisenhower administration, were now backing away from appointments:

> In 1953, the business executive found excitement in the prospect of a big job in the new Eisenhower administration. A crusade had just been won at the polls. A new program was to change the economic face of America. A "businessman's administration" was taking over. There was no trouble in filling jobs. Now, scarcely four years later, many of the 1953 appointees have gone back to private life, some of them deeply disillusioned. A new situation prevails. The President still wants brains, ability, experience in the top jobs. Now, however, he finds it very difficult to persuade men of such caliber to join his "team." He has trouble filling even cabinet posts. It takes a long time to find a qualified man who will accept a sub-cabinet position.[1]

---

[1] *U.S. News and World Report* (Aug. 9, 1957), p. 88.

The Eisenhower administration was not the first to encounter a serious shortage of able executives willing to accept political appointments. Actually, "every recent administration has experienced difficulty in filling its political executive positions on a satisfactory basis and in keeping them filled on such a basis."[2] The Task Force on Personnel of the second Hoover Commission traced these difficulties to four factors:

1. The shortage of persons possessing both well-developed executive ability and well-developed qualities of political leadership;

2. The failure to develop systematically in American life the capacities which are essential in political executives;

3. The difficulties and disadvantages suffered by executives who shuttle back and forth between public office and private life; and

4. Psychological and financial barriers to a ready interchange between a career in politics and a career in business.[3]

This shortage has probably become more serious in recent years. Increasingly the federal government relies on men of executive ability to make financial sacrifices for the purpose of serving the public on a volunteer, semicharitable basis. But clearly "the business of Government is not a part-time affair, nor a simple undertaking to be trusted to a parade of 'promising young executives.' "[4] The public, including the business community, has complacently al-

[2] Paul T. David and Ross Pollock, *Executives for Government* (1957), p. 10. See Chapter 2 for a discussion of the supply of qualified political executives for government service.

[3] U.S. Commission on Organization of the Executive Branch of the Government, *Task Force Report on Personnel and Civil Service* (1955), pp. 40-42.

[4] John J. Corson, "To Get Better Men for a Better Government," *New York Times Magazine* (March 27, 1949), p. 11.

lowed the supply of executive talent in the government to
erode away, with a crippling loss of trained personnel.
What can be done to bring qualified political executives
into the government? What are the principal deterrents
that keep executives from accepting political appointments
or discourage them from remaining in government service?
How can the supply of executives be increased in the near
future? It was to these questions that the Round Table
turned next.

WHAT BRINGS POLITICAL EXECUTIVES
INTO GOVERNMENT

It is relatively simple to identify a number of factors that
induce persons to accept positions as federal political executives, but it is difficult to weigh the relative importance
of these factors and to generalize about motivations that
bring executives into government service.

Personal Motives. Among important motivating factors may be included the following: opportunity for public
service; opportunity for self-development or self-fulfillment; opportunity to pursue political objectives; opportunity for more interesting and stimulating work; opportunity to improve career prospects outside of government
with government experience; desire for prestige, esteem,
or deference; desire to be influential in public affairs and
occupy a position of power; and pressures and urgings of
friends and high political leaders to accept a position.

A businessman with little or no previous government or
political involvement may be attracted by the personality of
the President and a desire to further the objectives of the
administration. A specialist or technician as distinguished
from an executive with a broad general outlook may be in-

terested in a political appointment in order to win esteem in his profession. The crusader, either from inside or outside the government, may want to perform a public service by overhauling a governmental program or by charting a new direction for public policy. A career executive may look forward to a political position as a logical evolution of his professional career or as a way of pursuing personal or political objectives. State and local governmental officials may accept appointment in Washington as an opportunity for more interesting or influential work. Any one of these types may be motivated to some extent by a desire to engage in a public service activity and at the same time to enhance his reputation in his local community, his industry, or among his associates.

A long-time observer of the Washington scene warned against easy generalizations about the factors that induce a man to accept a political post:

> A great deal depends on the character of the environment and the nature of the last election. My impression is that public service motivations are rather weak except during periods of national crisis. In emergency periods the public service appeal is very strong. I suspect that in 1933 Mr. Roosevelt could have gotten almost anybody, and again in 1939. But in between many people found it possible to resist a presidential appeal to come to serve in Washington. I am pretty sure there were many times when Mr. Truman couldn't get many of the people he wanted. I suspect that Mr. Eisenhower could have gotten almost anybody in 1953, but his batting average is not nearly as great today. Businessmen are less accustomed to public service in Washington than other groups in the population are. Consequently, a Republican administration that relies mainly on businessmen to serve as political executives may have to rely more on the personal pulling power of the President.

In a recent survey of business executives who held high-level posts in the federal government, the National Civil Service League found that patriotic appeals and the pull of public service are significant factors in bringing men into executive posts only in emergency periods. In 1952 a poll of 180 businessmen with government experience showed that 70 per cent reported that patriotism was a significant incentive only when the country was in real danger. Only 30 per cent felt that patriotism was an adequate incentive in normal periods. Other influences were prestige appeals, requests by high officials, urgings of friends and colleagues, examples of important business leaders, and the opportunity to broaden one's contacts. In a period of cutbacks in civilian business, the appeal of a government job was enhanced.[5] One participant discussed the range of motivating factors:

> Some people are influenced strongly by notions of what constitutes the public good. When these notions are also bound up with loyalty to a political party that happens to be in power in the White House, a call to serve in the administration is difficult to resist. Some people are also pleased enormously by the prospect of being an assistant secretary or under secretary in a department. It is a natural human desire to sit in a position of power. If such an opportunity is also portrayed as an opportunity to serve the country and to save it from political ruin, the incentive to accept appointment is pretty powerful.
>
> There seems to be an almost universal human appetite for deference and esteem. Now maybe the political executive in Washington really ought to expect very little deference from his fellow Americans, but the man who comes

[5] National Civil Service League, "The National Civil Service League's Survey of Business Executives Who Have Held High-Level Government Administrative Posts," mimeo., 1952.

here from Pocatello or Spokane and returns as an ex-assist-
ant secretary of a cabinet department probably gets a lot of
esteem. Assistant secretaries may be a dime a dozen in
Washington but not in Spokane.

For some people more than a desire for power, influence,
and esteem is needed. For some, service as a political executive may be a matter of self-fulfillment. They are attracted
by the opportunity to play a part in the larger problems
confronting American society and the free world.

Another observer commented:

I don't want to be cynical, but I remember a friend of
mine who said before the invention of radar that there was
no listening device in the world as delicate, sensitive, and
appreciative of the slightest sound as the ear of the aspirant
for public office listening for the call to duty.

The Presidential Appeal. The Round Table emphasized
the significance of the influence and pressure of friends and
key political leaders as factors motivating acceptance of
political executive appointments. The following interchange took place in the discussions:

The pressure of friends to accept appointment can be
very powerful. It is the obligation to others that brings
many people into government.

In some instances, top political executives are brought
into government by having the President call them up and
say, "I want you." President Roosevelt used to use this to
a greater degree than Eisenhower does. This is a form of
pressure that is very difficult to resist.

It is very difficult to resist if you feel any pull to perform
public service. If you don't have any particular internal
feeling about obligation to perform public service, it probably doesn't work well.

But if the president of your corporation tells you to go, you go.

It depends a great deal on the time and the environment. In wartime, it is one thing, and in peacetime it is quite another.

The appeal of a President is still almost irresistible, even from a Republican administration to a life-long Democrat. If the President of the United States sees a job for an individual to do and will go to the extent of personally inviting him to talk with him about it, it is mighty hard to turn the President down.

If the President of the United States personally and directly asks you, even in peacetime, to come to Washington, I doubt whether many would find it possible to refuse. But there is a limit to the time the President can take to recruit political executives. He certainly cannot recruit all or most of them. He must limit himself to cabinet and subcabinet positions.

Probably this power cannot be transferred from the President to anybody else. This makes it difficult for those who don't get in to see the President directly.

I think in the Roosevelt administration any number of people were told confidentially and in a low voice that "the President wants you to do this." But they subsequently discovered after some time on the job that the President didn't even know they existed.

Even the presidential appeal has its limitations:

Two conditions seem to be necessary if a presidential appeal is to succeed. First, the individual must agree with the basic principles that the administration is trying to promote insofar as they affect the particular job in question. Second, the individual must feel that the job is a feasible one. I know of instances when certain persons rejected presidential appeals because they felt that they were not in sympathy with the general policies of the administration as they affected the job or that the legislation setting up the agency was so inadequate that the job could not really be handled effectively.

Another member added:

I am wondering if there is not a third condition, which is a feeling by the person being recruited that the President is not saying this to everybody. The President must not say it too often. The fellow needs to feel that he is about the only one in town getting the call from the President. He may not know there were many others until he actually gets on the job.

A political executive told how he was recruited into government.

I was sitting quietly at my desk when a pleasant voice over the telephone said: "President Eisenhower has just returned from Korea. Would it be convenient for you to come over to see him tomorrow between 10 and 11?" I said it would, and the next day I fought my way through and finally got to see the President-elect. We were all alone. He said: "When we were on the battleship going from Guam to Hawaii, I was discussing my team and your name came up. I would be flattered if you would become a member of my team." Those were his exact words.

I happened to have known the President when he was President of Columbia University. I have always felt that the President of the United States should have any help he asks for. I also feel that the opportunity to pursue political objectives, especially when you have a change of administrations, is very important. I wanted to see the Eisenhower administration succeed. Nevertheless, I demurred and said I thought I could do much more for the President on the outside.

So I dismissed all thought of going down to Washington—but not altogether, because I was watching one position that I knew the President wanted to fill in a special field. I watched this spot for four months. Then I had a wire from Secretary ————— that reached me in California. It said: "Will you have lunch with me?" I went to Washington to see him and have lunch. He said to me: "You cannot escape any longer. You have got to help the President." He got in touch with the President and arranged for me to see him the next day.

After that I spent an hour with Sherman Adams, who gave me a pep talk. Then he said, "George Humphrey wants to see you." The Secretary of the Treasury was waiting for me. He said to me: "I want you to write down what I am going to tell you: It is your duty to come down here and stay as long as you are needed." Well, I didn't have to write it even once. I surrendered right then and there.

In my case, personal acquaintance with the President was a very strong factor. . . . I was so enamored with wanting to see the administration succeed that I was willing to come down to scrub floors. Had the President been a stranger to me, this appeal probably would not have worked. It was mainly my friendship with him and my strong support of his political ideals. I wanted to have a part in making those ideals work effectively.

A second political executive described his recruitment into government service:

I suppose I have served under a Democratic President more than I have under a Republican President. I didn't know either of them. Moreover I had never been involved in politics before and I didn't know the head of the department that I eventually went to work for. But I do know this. I sat across the table from President Eisenhower, who asked me if I thought I owed something to the United States. Well, I don't care if you are career or political, or a close friend or a complete unknown to the President. It makes little difference whether you agree or disagree with the President's philosophy. If you are asked that question and then are asked to do a job, I just don't think it is possible to refuse.

Now, a lot of other things enter into this recruiting process. I was at the time in an age bracket that put me probably at the height of my earning power. Nevertheless, I felt that I could never quite live with myself if I said no. If you are in a war or in a critical situation, you cannot help feeling a terrific personal and selfish satisfaction in being sought out personally by the President of the United States.

A Round Table participant suggested that it is important to consider the related question of the compensations that accrue after leaving a government position:

A friend of mine left after ten years of public service in one of the new agencies. He was in his mid-forties and held a rather responsible job. He is now back practicing law very successfully in Wall Street. I saw him about six months later and asked him how he felt about his ten years in Washington. He said: "I look back on it with the satisfaction that while I was at the height of my powers, such as they are, even though I was wielding a very small brush, I was painting on a very large canvas." This comment has been expressed to me many times by executives who have performed well in their posts.

The opportunity for stimulating work might serve as a stronger incentive to accept political appointment in Wash-

ington if businessmen and other potential candidates for
these positions were more familiar with political processes
and governmental operations. Those who accept and stay
for a while in such positions learn to value the psychic income derived from them. As a Round Table participant
stated on an earlier occasion:

> Many businessmen who served in the WPB, the War
> Department or elsewhere during the war experienced a
> letdown upon their return to private business. They had
> felt the thrill of dealing with national affairs. They enjoyed
> "doing their bit," contributing even slightly to the national
> welfare. They learned how infinitely complex the conduct
> of the public business can be. And when they returned,
> they found their old civilian jobs . . . dull and uninterest-
> ing.[6]

Some Cautionary Comments.   Another member of the
Round Table recalled his transfer from a career to a political executive position:

> One afternoon in September 1946, I was sitting in the
> Bureau of the Budget in a nice, safe Grade 15 job. I was
> called on the phone successively first by the assistant secre-
> tary of Commerce, then by the assistant secretary of the
> Navy, the assistant secretary of State, and finally the chair-
> man of the Civil Aeronautics Board, to put the heat on me
> to take a job that I finally took.
> This situation produced a small crisis for me. The new
> job was temporary as far as anybody could see, and I even-
> tually ascertained that the Budget Bureau would not give
> me a leave. But by that time I had become so committed
> that I could not gracefully withdraw from my tentative

[6] Corson, "To Get Better Men for a Better Government," *op. cit.,*
p. 48.

willingness to take the other job, and began preparing to resign. Then I discovered that a prominent political executive was doing his best to blackball the appointment. So I was embarrassed from all sides.

Eventually the political difficulties were straightened out and I took the job. I suppose I will never really know what were the controlling reasons that led me to do so. There was no significant pay difference and less security. I was certainly tired of the anonymity of the civil service staff job, and there was nothing anonymous about the hot political spot I went into.

A former political executive urged the Round Table to guard against too lofty a view of the incentives that bring men into political executive posts:

I must admit that my views on executive recruitment have become a bit sordid. In 1952, many people were attracted to the Eisenhower administration on the basis of an opportunity to associate themselves with the President and with a philosophy they adhered to deeply. But there was also a great number of men who sought political appointments pretty vigorously on a rather crass, commercial basis. They regarded government service as a chance to develop a reputation, to make contacts they could capitalize on later on. I don't want to overstate this element, but it is a part of the process.

We need to avoid glorifying the fellow who accepts political appointment. I think there is a call to public service which is meaningful, particularly when voiced by the President; but a lot of other practical or materialistic considerations influence decisions to accept appointment.

Another former executive added:

I don't want to single out any particular group or profession, but we would all probably agree that government service is no penalty in the legal profession. There are all sorts of advantages to be gained professionally by lawyers working in the government. More often it has been the lawyer rather than the businessman who has found it to his advantage to be identified as a government official and to become better known through his associations here.

Several members of the Round Table stressed the importance of the Business Advisory Council of the Department of Commerce as a recruiting mechanism for cabinet and sub-cabinet positions as well as for heads of divisions and specialists in civilian defense agencies. One member said:

As an institution, I would suspect that the Business Advisory Council over the last two decades has brought as many people into top positions in the government as almost any other single agency. Some of these people took jobs later on because they had become acquainted with the opportunities of government work and saw that things they were interested in could be accomplished here. But others came in because presidents and vice presidents of corporations, who were members of the council, agreed to make some of their best men available to the government during World War II, the Korean period, and later. In the first instance, the council was the source of supply itself. In the second, it was the recruiting agent. The present administration has used it to fill positions at the assistant secretary level. Moreover, Mr. Humphrey, Mr. Wilson, and other members of the Eisenhower Cabinet were members of the BAC before they joined the government.[7]

[7] For an account of some of the activities and personnel of the Business Advisory Council see U.S. House Committee on the Judiciary, *Interim Report of the Antitrust Subcommittee on "The Business Advisory Council for the Department of Commerce"* (1955).

Some further light can be shed on the problem of improving the supply of political executives by noting the major deterrents to acceptance of political appointments.

WHY POLITICAL APPOINTMENTS ARE REFUSED

In his book, *Executives for the Federal Service,* John Corson summarized the reasons most often given by 80 per cent of those who refused government appointments during the Korean emergency.[8] They included: inadequate compensation; inability to leave private affairs; insecurity; abuse of public officials; and fear of legal reprisal growing out of possible violation of "conflict of interest" statutes.

Some Practical Considerations. In the Round Table discussions Mr. Corson commented on developments in executive recruitment since 1952:

Since I wrote that book, I have had one substantial experience that gives me a little more realistic understanding of the problem. This was the experience of working with the group around Mr. Eisenhower in 1952 which tried to determine how much of a recruitment problem the new administration would have. We tried to define the policy jobs in the new administration and then to develop lists of names to fill all those jobs. I had an opportunity to work with two of the cabinet secretaries. My task was to follow up on some of these names in order to find out if they were good prospects for executive posts.

On the basis of this experience, I would be inclined to say that the abuse of public officials and fear of legal reprisals are still talked about a good deal but are not really major deterrents any more. The real objections to taking an

[8] See Chap. 4.

executive job in Washington are: inadequate compensation, inability to leave private affairs, and insecurity. Their relative significance depends upon the age and situation of the individual. Security means quite a bit to the fellow who is 40 and just on the threshold of an important career in his company, but it does not mean much to a man who is 55 or 60 and is looking for a change of pace and something to cap his career with.

As I read the reasons why many people refuse to take these jobs, I would emphasize the so-called practical ones— the inadequate pay, the inability of a corporate executive who is on the way up the promotional ladder to leave his job because he doesn't want to endanger his pension rights and is fearful that others in the corporation will take his place in the corporation if he leaves. These are practical matters of great importance today.

I would also attach some importance to rather personal factors. Some men find it very difficult for family reasons to break away from their corporate environment in order to move to Washington. The interests and desires of wives and children are given considerable weight. On the other hand, some men may find it advantageous to break ties for a while, especially to take a position abroad. The experience of close friends and the example of prominent business leaders are relevant here. If business friends and associates have had constructive experiences in their tours of duty in government positions, a fellow is likely to be influenced in a positive way to accept political appointment. But if these experiences have been frustrating or otherwise unfortunate, and if the return to private life was less than wholly satisfactory, the deterring influence is strong indeed.

Under present pay schedules, it is impossible for the government to compete directly with private business for executive talent. As a close student of the problem has noted:

> Most recruiting for top talent [in the government] proceeds on the assumption that if an executive in industry will accept a paid public position at all, he will be prepared to do so at some financial sacrifice. In many cases, however, the difficulty arises from the fact that the individual has built up personal financial commitments that make it virtually impossible for him to accept a salary rate at the government level.[9]

Maintaining two separate residences on a reduced salary plus the high cost of living and social obligations in Washington keep many younger family men out of Washington. A reporter's inquiry in 1957 indicated that "coming to Washington" means taking a cut in income that involves more than the immediate loss of pay:

> Recently, the secretary of a large department needed a man to fill an important policy-administrative post. After some search, his eye fell on a young executive coming up fast in a big automobile company. The cabinet official quickly won approval from the company's president to "borrow" the prospect. But when he talked to the man himself, the secretary just as quickly met resistance. In addition to the cut in salary, the fellow worried that he might lose his place in the escalator that ten years from now would land him in the front office, or near it. He thought it over. In the end the promise of security of staying at home outweighed the "honor and opportunity" of public service in Washington. He decided to "play safe," and the secretary looked elsewhere to fill his spot.[10]

[9] Paul T. David, "The Development and Recruitment of Administrative Leadership in National and International Programs," Robert A. Walker, ed., *America's Manpower Crisis* (1952), p. 149.

[10] Jay Walz, "Help Wanted: Top Men for Washington," *New York Times Magazine* (Oct. 13, 1957), p. 24.

In 1954 *Fortune* called attention to the same problem:

> For the young man whose fame and fortune lie ahead, and for the older man whose fame and fortune are already established, even a four-year tour in Washington might be attractive. But for the business executive in the prime of his career, an extended non-emergency tour in Washington is a contradiction of his apparent personal aims. His dispensability to his corporation and his corporation's indispensability to him are bound to remain the crux of his problem.[11]

A slowing down in the movement from private life to government and back to private life troubled the Round Table. One participant reported:

> There seems to be a growing rigidity in our social structure that makes it increasingly difficult for the government to recruit competent executives from business, universities, and other areas of private activity. We seem to be moving in a direction in which government and business personnel, except in a very limited sense, will not be interchangeable.

Another member stated:

> In industry, we have a society that is becoming increasingly stabilized in its structure. In industry more than in academic life, a man is on an administrative ladder of progress that leaves him little flexibility in his career plans if he wants to stay with the company. In academic life, a fellow can go out for a year and come right back to teach the same courses and handle the same laboratories. When four out of five people work for somebody else, usually a large corporation, they have to stay in that hierarchy or they are not going to climb the ladder.

[11] John McDonald, "The Businessman in Government," *Fortune*, Vol. 50 (July 1954), p. 158.

Fifty to a hundred years ago, perhaps four out of five people were self-employed. You could come down to Congress and serve a term and go back home and be a country lawyer or open up a general store. Today these shifts are much more difficult to manage. Even the lawyer is less attracted to government service today. Society itself may be more mobile but the fellow on the make somewhere below the top of the executive ladder cannot move around much except within his own company or industry.

It is the rigidity at the top that worries me. More and more, the way a fellow holds on to the opportunity to compete for an executive position is by staying in that corporation where he already has an established position.

The Lack of Prestige. The relatively low prestige of governmental activity still represents a significant deterrent in keeping people out of government. A participant explained:

> One of the amazing things about service in Washington is that you can leave town and within hours be with a group of former associates who couldn't care less about government. Not only are they ignorant of your problems, but they don't really get emotionally involved in any way. To them it is a popular sport to criticize government.

> Back in the early days of the New Deal, government really provided a wonderful opportunity for people who felt they could do something constructive and significant in government. Undoubtedly the availability of government jobs in a period of deep unemployment had something to do with this situation also. In any case, I imagine that this positive and enthusiastic approach to government has not been duplicated since. Perhaps there was a little when President Eisenhower took office, but the goal of the new administration was mainly to throw the Democratic rascals out. With the exception of the social planners, who get up

a head of steam on their mission in fair weather and foul, these conditions come and go with the times, as it did with the New Deal and during the first few months of the Eisenhower administration.

What concerns me the most is the lack of concern, almost the unwillingness to debate questions related to the purposes of government. When a fellow is asked to accept a political appointment in Washington, he may wonder whether it is a good thing for him to associate himself with a government that many of his associates regard as a great spending machine that is eating away the vitals of our liberties.

Another participant added:

We are living in a free enterprise economy in which the businessman forms the dominant group. More often than not, the businessman is looked to as the trustee of American society. He is, in our scheme of things, the respected and honored figure. The young fellow coming out of college today is looking forward to a position that the community respects and esteems; he is considering what he wants to be twenty years from now. The overwhelming majority of these fellows do not consider a career in politics or in government service.

The Loyalty-Security Issue.   The Round Table believed that by 1957 the adverse pressures of the security program in federal employment had tapered off and no longer constituted a serious deterrent to recruitment at both career and political levels.

In 1953 and 1954, several solid backbone Republicans for four or five generations refused to come to Washington to take their chances with McCarthyism. They simply said: "Having a liberal streak somewhere along the line while you are in college is like growing up and wearing your first bow tie." The security programs did a lot of damage to the federal service, including the top executive levels as well as the career area at all salary levels. But they mellowed quite a bit beginning in 1955. It is hardly a factor at all in our present recruitment of executives.

Some members of the Round Table were not so sanguine about the latter-day effects of McCarthyism:

I am astonished if loyalty-security matters no longer have an adverse effect on the federal service. Perhaps we are now getting out of the age brackets during which these questionable personal records were made. But I ran across a couple of stories in the early days of the Eisenhower administration where men of absolutely impeccable respectability had been picked by the presidents of their companies to volunteer for public service. In these cases, they had extreme difficulty because the government raised questions about their memberships in some doubtful organization when they were juniors in college. They wanted to have their names withdrawn from consideration because they much preferred not to face up to the facts of their college associations.

One participant asserted:

Today the security officers seem to be concerned not so much with possible disloyalty or security risks but rather with the personality and social habits of candidates and incumbents. They want to know what organizations they belonged to or whether they went to football games and got drunk or went around with what they now consider to be the wrong people.

Another member explained:

There may be no problem any more on security matters for college graduates entering the government at the junior grades. They belong to a college generation that is scarcely tempted to belong to off-color organizations. The extreme left-wing groups have been so discredited that college students have stayed away in droves. But for the fellow who grew out of adolescence in the late twenties and 1930's, there is still some problem.

Conflicts of Interest.   Among the many restraints on federal employees are a number of laws that have come to be known as the "conflict-of-interest" laws. The term does not appear in the law books at all. These "conflict-of-interest" laws are Sections 216, 281, 283, 284, 434, and 1914 of Title 18 of the U.S. Criminal Code and Section 99 of Title 5 (Executive Departments and Agencies) of the U.S. Code. Five of them apply to the conduct of all government employees during their public service, and two restrict their activity after they have left the government. Only one of the laws applies to members of Congress.

In brief, the statutes forbid present and former government employees from engaging in certain activities that might lead to a conflict between their duty to the public and their private interests. Two of the laws prevent government employees from receiving certain forms of nongovernment income. Section 1914 forbids the receipt by a government employee from an outside source of "any salary in connection with his government service." Section 434 forbids a government employee from transacting business on behalf of the government with any firm in which he has a "pecuniary interest."

Section 216 forbids a government employee from receiving compensation for procuring a government contract for an outside interest. Section 283 forbids a government employee from prosecuting claims against the government, gratuitously or for pay. Section 281 forbids congressmen and employees of the executive and judicial branches from receiving money for performing any services of any kind before the government for an outside interest. For a period of two years after his government employment has ended, an official is forbidden by Section 284 of Title 18 and Section 99 of Title 5 from prosecuting certain claims against the government.

In addition to these statutes, special laws apply to particular positions and offices. Furthermore, many agencies have adopted their own rules, and the Senate applies its own standards in considering the confirmation of presidential appointments.

The Round Table was somewhat divided on the deterrent effects of conflicts of interest upon recruitment of political executives.

According to a Department of Defense executive:

> The conflict of interest statutes cause us more trouble in recruiting than any other single thing, including inadequate salary. Some time ago, several executives in the department divided up a list of 57 names to fill an important executive post. We felt that any one on the list would be all right. We were not successful. In about half of the cases, conflict of interest under the statutes kept us from getting men who otherwise would have been willing to come to Washington for two or four years. We have to find a better solution to this problem to enable the department to get its fair share of executive talent.
>
> We recently had a difficult job in research development to fill. Person after person declined the job because of conflict of interest. One fellow we wanted badly had several thousand shares of stock in a company he had worked in for 35 years. He is good for at least a few more years of

executive work. He would love to come to Washington, but he will not sell his stock in order to do so.

We have to find a solution to the conflict of interest problem. I think we could develop a standard of ethical behavior in this area that could be incorporated in the law and be made to work.

A nongovernmental executive pointed out that it was not enough for government officials to be sure that their colleagues were not influenced by their continuing business associations and interests:

> The public as well as the government must be assured that its officials are acting in the best interest of the public at all times. If we loosen the provisions of the conflict of interest statutes a great deal, we run the risk of never being sure when a fellow is allowing his private interests to guide his public judgment. If a fellow from the railroad industry continues to hold stock in a particular railroad company, it would be possible for him to abstain on matters that involve that company. But how could you be sure that he would not be influenced by his former railroad connections in certain broad policy matters where his former company was not directly involved?

The Round Table agreed that conflicts of interest produced problems for corporations as well as for individuals. As one political executive stated:

> The other side of the coin there is the problem of the ethical corporations. They want to avoid any possible charge that one of their former executives or one of their men on leave with the government is there primarily to look out for their corporate interests. The companies that employ executives who had real trouble with conflict of interest statutes have become gun shy. They don't want to

run the risk of notoriety and bad publicity reflecting on the integrity of the corporation by exposing more of their top executives to the scrutiny of reporters and congressmen in Washington. Many companies are very reluctant to tell any of their men to accept positions with a government department. They want to avoid a subsequent charge of conflict of interest that might reflect adversely on the company.

This problem affects not only the Department of Defense. It involves almost all departments and agencies filling jobs equivalent to assistant secretary posts. The unwillingness of corporations to face possible charges of conflict of interest has had the effect of drying up some of our sources of executive talent. The great majority of executives stay on the job for less than four years. When you add to the recruiting problem the deterrents of financial sacrifice and possible conflicts of interest, you reduce the already short supply of political executives.

Another participant provided additional documentation:

A personnel director of a large corporation wanted earnestly to accept appointment as an assistant secretary in a major department recently, but his company held back. The company said that under normal circumstances they would be happy to release the fellow for government service. But a short while ago a prominent congressman made a speech on the floor of the House calling attention in a derogatory way to the number of men who came from the company to work for the government in recent years. The company felt that it could not afford more adverse publicity that it would get by sending another of its executives to Washington.

The Round Table concluded that many corporations today discourage their personnel from going to work for the government because the corporations have been attacked in Congress and elsewhere for having too many people infiltrate into the government: "All this is to say that fewer companies are making people available to government today."

A member of the Round Table summarized the major deterrents keeping able businessmen out of political executive posts:

> We have identified three types of deterrents of major importance. The first is the reluctance of younger executives in their 30's and 40's to leave the corporation ladder for fear of losing their places or sacrificing their pension rights. The second is the company's reluctance to let their top men accept government positions out of fear that the company may be embarrassed by future attacks or disqualify itself from doing business with the government in the future. Perhaps some of this reluctance stems from the unwillingness of the company to invest its funds in the fringe benefits it maintains for staff on leave with the government. And the third type of deterrent is the conflict of interest between the executive's private interests and his public responsibility.

WHY POLITICAL APPOINTEES LEAVE

The reasons offered for leaving political executive positions are legion. Among those most often referred to are unwillingness to continue making financial sacrifices, the frustration growing out of lack of success in getting things done quickly in a complicated and unfamiliar environment, congressional buffeting and harassment, and the necessity to get back on the promotion ladder in private careers. To these can be added such factors as family pressure, loss of political support in the administration, unreconciled policy controversies, existence of strong specialist and other staff views that block the achievement of broad objectives, as defined by political executives, conflict of interest problems, and the receipt of compelling offers of attractive positions elsewhere. For example, as one participant reported:

In a major department in 1956, there was a complete turnover of top staff excluding the secretary himself. Three assistant and under secretaries left, and three came to take their places. Two of the men left mainly because of inadequate income. The third one left because he is essentially in the category of the fellow who is on his way up in his organization and he could not afford to stay out any longer. Of the two fellows that the department tried unsuccessfully to hire, one was not in a position to leave his company, which had been criticized for loaning too many executives to the government; while the other one was really on the make in his company and couldn't take the chance of leaving. One of the incumbents left to go back to his university. Think of it—back to his university for more money!

Perhaps the most obvious reason why political executives leave their posts is that they never intended to stay for more than a short time in the first place. The Round Table estimated that the departures of one half to two thirds of all political executives can be explained by the fact that they came into government with short-term commitments. As one participant stated:

This suggests that the people complaining about heavy turnover among political executives should complain instead about the terms under which they were originally recruited. On the other hand, to expect these fellows to stay much longer than they do is very difficult. They give up a good deal to come and feel that they have to go back.

Another member said: "We are not looking for political executives on a long term basis today. We just borrow them for a short while from private life. Therefore, some of these considerations as to why people leave the service are irrelevant."

RECRUITMENT FOR THE CAREER SERVICE

By and large career executives in the federal government are recruited originally in the lowest professional levels of the federal service.

Importance of Recruiting Juniors.   One career executive noted:

From the standpoint of my agency, the kind of people we recruit in the GS-5 grade is tremendously important to its future. Since we rarely take people in the top levels from industry, we look to our civil service juniors for executive talent. The number one motivation that we depend on to get good young people into the agency is money. Last year the universities were deluged with scouts looking for likely employees in the senior class. The students being interviewed are interested mainly in immediate salary, and a differential of $25 or $50 a month was often the determining factor in the fellow's decision. These college seniors today are not interested in retirement plans. I have tried to sell them on that and have gotten nowhere fast. They are much more interested in any plan that will enable them to provide for their families in case they get hurt or killed.

Apart from salary questions these college seniors seem to be vitally affected by the prestige of a government agency. They are concerned not so much with the prestige of the government as a whole but rather with the standing of a particular agency. They want to be part of an organization that is accomplishing something useful. All of these things, which are immediate and present rather than in the future, seem to mean more to them than anything else. These are the men who eventually rise to career grades and become career executives.

The Round Table explored reasons why top career people stay with the government instead of taking jobs in industry. A career executive in a scientific service responded: "I can only speak for the medical and biological sciences, and here nothing holds on to the career executives. They don't stay." A second answered:

My agency employs thousands of people, and we have to have a dedicated body of career people to keep it going. But they are all different. Some have had little professional training but have become expert in certain fields as they have gained experience. Some of them can hold their own with highly paid lawyers and accountants representing private companies. They stay with us in some cases because they do not have the personality to go out and get clients. Another type of career man has a retentive memory that stores up an amazing collection of facts. This fellow often is an extrovert but without the personality that instills confidence in others. Frequently this sort of fellow stays with us because he lacks the confidence in himself that he needs to go out on his own.

Perhaps the one thing that keeps many of our fine people in the service is the lack of confidence in themselves to cut loose from the government and make their way in a competitive environment. They lack a rounded ability. The same sort of condition can be found in banking, insurance, and public utility companies generally. A fellow gets accustomed to a big organization and his place in it and he doesn't like to pull out.

Another participant noted an additional factor that helps to keep career people on the job:

> When I looked into this question a short time ago, I wrote to several score men in GS-15 and GS-16 jobs. One of them wrote back very frankly to say that there was a very simple reason why he has not left the government: "I have never been offered an opportunity." Many people in the federal government are just not exposed to opportunities to get out. They don't have contact with people who might serve as future clients of a lawyer or accountant in private practice, or they do not meet with representatives of industries looking for able people.

Still another reported:

> There is a truism worth remembering here. In general people enjoy doing things in which they excel. They get into a federal job and get accustomed to it. They are often in jobs that have no counterparts in private life. They feel a sense of comfort in performing a job well that they have learned to do. They do one job well and get promoted to the next level and so forth. This is the way of life for a great many people who are some of the best civil servants we have.

Recruiting from Outside Government.   In an expanding organization, it may not be possible to fill top positions from within the agency. An executive in a scientific bureau reported considerable difficulties in this type of recruitment:

> Our agency needed some top administrative people with technical training, and we did not have enough candidates already on our staff. So we looked around for more candidates. In recruiting for these jobs, we found that it was

not so much the money that deterred many from accepting appointment to career jobs.

For example, one fellow turned me down today. I asked if it was the salary. He said that it was about $1,000 less than he was now getting, but that in itself was not very important to him. He said: "I don't think I can get along well in government service. More so than in my university job, a career executive in government has to fight and die for everything he gets, and the struggle is never over. It goes on at successively higher levels again and again. After being in government during the war, I feel that I don't want to go through this sort of trial by combat again."

This fellow also reported that he did not want his programs influenced unduly by forces he regarded as irrelevant, for example, a disagreement between a chairman and several ranking members of a congressional committee that resulted in long delays in considering certain legislative proposals affecting a program. This fellow also felt that, as a trained professional in a specialized area, he could not afford to let his special skill deteriorate while serving in an administrative capacity. He felt that administrative duties would prevent him from keeping up with his professional work. This last point is very important in a scientific program. Some of our best administrators in scientific programs go to pot because they feel that, as administrators, they are no longer engaged in a scientific endeavor. They resent giving up the working clothes of the laboratory scientist for the dress of an office administrator.

The Round Table noted that it is more difficult to appeal to a university man than a businessman on public service grounds to accept a career position.

You go fishing in a very tough place when you go to a

university instead of a private business to find candidates for a career position. The university man is already in a kind of public service. On the other hand, a man who is in private business and has made a lot of money may occasionally feel a primal urge to do something for society and for the community. The note of public service may work with this kind of fellow.

Obstacles to recruitment of career executives from outside the government have forced most government agencies to develop their career executives from among the best talent available in the government. As one executive stated: We have an extensive program to build up our best career people by identifying them as early as possible and giving them opportunities to enrich their experience. On the other hand, heavy reliance on internal recruitment may be hazardous. One participant put it this way:

If you rely entirely upon developing your own executives in the career service, you risk developing a bureaucracy that is isolated and insulated from the community at large. The purpose of recruiting career executives at the intermediate or top level from the outside is to bring a fresh point of view into the bureaucracy. It also gives a fellow who may eventually go back to private life a better understanding of public affairs.

Repeatedly the Round Table expressed a desire for greater interchange of personnel at executive levels between government and business, both for career and for political posts. The prospects, however, appeared dim. One member explained:

We have almost two separate worlds of government and business that are divided to a much greater degree than many of our discussions reflect. In several agencies a high proportion of people in Grade 15 positions and above joined the government service during the New Deal period or during World War II and have had no other employer. This situation illustrates the lack of interchange between business and government.

The Continuing Shortage.   A career executive referred to disturbing trends in his bureau:

> My bureau is strictly a career organization; recruitment for the highest career posts is entirely from within. I am not sure that this situation will continue. In an economy of full employment, we are getting more competition from private industry than we used to get. As a result, some of our good people are leaving. Some of those who leave are very disappointed later on because they miss the feeling of responsibility and the satisfaction of accomplishment they associated with their government positions.
>
> Nevertheless, we probably will have to continue to recruit our career executives from within. Unless we get more and better people in at the bottom of the professional ladder, we are going to have a smaller group of people to recruit from in the future. We are now facing up to the fact that somewhere along the line in the middle grades competent men are moving out. In other words, we are having difficulty getting people at the bottom, and we are losing people in the middle grades just when they have really established themselves as potential executives.

Another career executive commented similarly:

> I am really alarmed about the supply of career executives in the federal government. The quality of the material available for promotion to the top is nothing like what it was in the 1930's and early 1940's. Yet the times de-

mand even greater skills and a substantially increased number. In my judgment, we are falling down badly in recruiting potential career executives and developing them in a systematic way.

IMPROVING THE SUPPLY OF EXECUTIVES

In its search for ways to improve the supply of political and career executives, the Round Table dealt mainly with three possibilities: greater reliance on political parties as sources of executive talent, efforts to make executive posts more attractive, and improved personnel practices.

Can the Parties Help? Can the political parties do a better job of supplying competent political executives? Generally the Round Table was very skeptical about the possibility. One career executive speculated whether the parties had a definite obligation to provide more qualified candidates for political executive posts:

> In my talks with party leaders, I usually find agreement that the party machinery ought to contribute to the supply of qualified executives, but rarely have I found anyone willing to take some concrete action. My impression is that there is less responsiveness by national party organizations now to the personnel problems of government than we had some years ago. Some state central committees have attempted to provide qualified candidates for political posts in the executive branches of state governments, but there is little carry-over from state party offices to national party committees. The state-local party organizations are in business continuously, preparing for some election. The national party machinery is a hollow shell compared to these state and local party organizations.

According to another member:

It is very doubtful whether any President or member of a cabinet can afford to delegate the recruiting job to a party system whose center of gravity lies at the state and local levels rather than the national level. Most members of the President's cabinet do not come up through the ranks of the party; they are inclined to look upon lists of candidates supplied by the national party machinery with great suspicion. What they want is competence, and some of them may think that competence and party activity are incompatible.

The experience of the Eisenhower administration offers little encouragement to those who hope for greater effectiveness from the national party machinery in locating and supplying political executives. One member of the Round Table described the early experience of the new administration:

In 1952, the President-elect and his staff began to identify the jobs they proposed to fill, department by department. They had a roster of more than 5,000 names, and a committee of distinguished Republicans reviewed the roster. It did not produce very well for the administration. Although almost every state party committee contributed to it, there was no follow through to the state committees beyond the mere production of names. There was very little information available on the availability of candidates. It was a shopping list of prospects only. The committee's operation of the roster lasted only about 6 months. It turned out that a number of cabinet secretaries had no intention of using the roster. They wanted to get their own men from nonpolitical sources.

Another was even more skeptical:

> Being on a party's shopping list is the best way to avoid appointment. The parties have no standards for judging competence in political executives, and those who have the primary voice in the appointing power will not use party lists. This is not the way political executives are hired in American politics. In any case there are real liabilities in a list of 5,000 or more names. There is nothing selective about that.

One member suggested that more attention be given to defeated candidates for elected office:

> Candidates for elective public office have already gone through the best training school we have for political executives. I don't know who invented the term "lame duck," but this term has become a smear phrase that has destroyed an available field of political prospects. If you presume that anybody defeated for elective office is no good, *per se,* you preclude a very valuable source of recruitment. But a man's defeat at the polls often has no relation to his political or administrative talents. I am astonished at the number of able people who are defeated for office and are allowed to go out of public life altogether because of some anxiety that the administration will be accused of filling the government with lame ducks. There should be no disgrace in electoral defeat.

Generally the Round Table concluded that the practice of American presidential government does not support the likelihood that the parties can be relied upon to supply useful candidates for political executive positions. A member explained:

> We would have to create a presidential party system

rather than the present alliance of state and local parties to make the parties effective recruiting agents. And we would have to have a much closer identification of cabinet members with the party machinery. There is no possibility of making these changes in the foreseeable future.

Making Jobs More Attractive.   Can executive positions for political and career officials be made more attractive? One career participant stated that one of the ways executive positions can be made more attractive is to provide for greater diversity in job assignments:

> We ought to rotate the assignments of an executive fairly often. We should also give him opportunities to serve on committees, not all of which fall in his area of special training or competence. In my 35 years in government service I have served on only one State Department committee that affected my work. I should have been given more opportunity to broaden my interests. We might keep the short-term executive on the job for a longer period if we gave him a change of pace in the nature of his responsibilities and give him challenging goals and incentives.

Another career executive proposed that careful attention be given to the development of appropriate forms of recognition for able executives:

> Take the British government. They send off a man to a remote part of the world, and underpay and frustrate him for 25 years. But in between, the Crown decorates him for distinguished public service and he stays on. He takes pride in it, and his family takes pride in him. We have not gone nearly far enough in the federal government in acknowledging and rewarding distinguished public service.[12]

[12] These statements were made before the Presidential citations of 1957-58.

A third career executive concurred:

The government's difficulties in holding on to its executives are not unlike the difficulties that occur in business. An executive, whether in private life or in government, wants recognition and the feeling of liking his associates and the work he is doing and being appreciated. A great deal can be done by an executive to develop loyalty in his top assistants, especially by getting to know them on a first-name basis, and in appreciating them.

Another added:

I had an illustration of this point the other day. A deputy commissioner of a very large bureau was looking for a corporate job. The secretary of the department told him that he was needed there, and that was enough to keep him. We do a lot of moaning around about some of our personnel problems, but some of the trouble we can cure ourselves with little or no expense.

Better Personnel Practices.   According to the Round Table, better personnel practices would ease the problem of recruiting and keeping able career executives. In particular, more skillful recruitment by political and career executives would help. As one career executive reported:

I receive many invitations to talk to professional graduate schools. I tell the students about the advantages of working for the government. My talk has a lot of anecdotes and amusing stories. I try to give them the feeling that the government is a decent, human sort of place to work. Frankly, I emphasized the advantages of government service and the weaknesses of employment in private industry.

We don't do nearly enough to recruit our staffs. For example, I know many men who have gone to work for private companies at $50 more per month than the government was paying. But few of these men have opportunities to broaden their interests. Many of them do today exactly what they did on the job several years ago. They have not progressed. One told me the other day: "There are few opportunities for me to rise in this company. I know the man above me and he knows me. But he has never called at my house. He has never met my family. The superintendent of the plant does not know my name."

The human touch counts for a great deal in government. I have been going out to visit our field offices and having meetings with our staffs. We also get together informally with their families. We cannot afford to gather at hotels, so we usually have a picnic out at some campground. And how I hate picnics! All the women bring some good food, but you have no idea how many kinds of potato salad there are in this world, and how many things you think and hope aren't potato salad but turn out to be potato salad anyway. The women watch you carefully to see whether you take some of their food. I try nobly to do the best I can. I gained 12 pounds on my last trip.

When I leave the picnic, I will be calling every fellow by his first name. Maybe you think this doesn't amount to much, but you would be awfully mistaken. Somehow this personal, intangible touch can be pretty constructive in solving some personnel problems.

A second career executive commented similarly:

I can tell you one experience about the importance of the wives of our employees. Our bureau publishes a little magazine that goes to all employees. In it I have discussed the propriety of the wives of our employees going through some of the institutions we manage to get better acquainted with their husbands' work. Soon we organized tours of the institutions for the women and gave brief lectures on how things were done. Surprisingly I received more letters of commendation from the wives for that little program than I ever did from their husbands. This training course for wives paid off very well.

Can some of the environmental hazards in American politics be minimized in order to make executive posts more attractive to qualified persons? The Round Table appeared to suggest that effective possibilities of altering some of the significant characteristics of the environment of federal executives were indeed remote. The Round Table hoped rather for a more sympathetic understanding of the peculiarities of the federal environment and the demands that it makes upon federal executives, and for more skill in handling the problems of recruitment and adjustment on the part of all concerned.

VIII

Orientation of New Executives

THE IRRELEVANCY of almost all nonfederal experience as preparation for an executive position in Washington has created one of the overriding personnel problems of recent Republican and Democratic administrations: the need for effective orientation. Generally speaking, most political executives and some career executives, particularly in emergency periods, are recruited from the business world, the universities, or other governments, with little or no previous contact with federal administration. For example, during World War II:

> The need for good men was partly satisfied by drawing on private business, but the effectiveness of these men as federal executives was often delayed and made more difficult by a common deficiency. Too many of them did not have an adequate appreciation of the special characteristics and problems of public administration and too few had any real working knowledge of governmental organization as a whole and the relationship of his department to others. This may have been the result of personal indifference or a lack in our system of education, or both. Whatever the reason, it made more work for everybody. The newly sworn-in administrator added much vitality to administration and he generally learned fast; but when he approached the job with the attitude that "everything

in government is terrible" and tried to run his office as he did when he was head of the National Bustle and Flute Corporation, he became a first-class headache.[1]

The persistent problem of filling top managerial posts in the federal government is complicated by the reluctance of political executives to remain on the job for more than two or three years. Between 1933 and 1952 the average tenure of departmental secretaries was three and one half years; under secretaries served just under two years; and assistant secretaries served for only two and two-thirds years on the average.[2] Under the Eisenhower administration, tenure in these positions from 1953 to 1958 tended to decline. The impact of high turnover on American politics has been suggested by a Washington reporter:

> In the forward echelons of government, including Cabinet and sub-Cabinet positions, there are 750 offices of exceptional political and executive responsibility. These jobs deal with continuing and long-range problems—national defense, foreign aid, atomic energy. They demand men of high talent, ingenuity and determination to foster and administer the programs by which the Administration stands or falls.
>
> Yet it is an accepted fact of life in Washington that fully one-third of the officials holding these posts today [October 1957] may be gone a year from now. In some agencies, including some of the more sensitive, the proportion of departees will be higher. But it is safe to say that, twelve months hence, 250 of these highest offices

[1] Robert A. Lovett, "A Business Executive Looks at Government," Joseph E. McLean, ed., *The Public Service and University Education* (1949), pp. 76-77.

[2] U.S. Commission on Organization of the Executive Branch of the Government, *Task Force Report on Personnel and Civil Service* (1955), p. 219. See also Chap. IV, p. 85 and Chap. V, pp. 92-93.

will probably be in new, and ofttimes inexperienced, hands. When one considers the cumulative effect of this turnover in two or three years, or in an Administration's four-year term of office, the results are startling.[3]

NEW EXECUTIVES IN A NEW ADMINISTRATION

The process of turning an inexperienced political executive into a productive and useful member of the President's corps of managers is particularly difficult for a new administration of a party coming into office for the first time in many years. The situation could scarcely have been more difficult than it was in 1953.

In many ways there were no real American precedents for the situation. The period of executive control by the outgoing party had been characterized by the unusual duration of 20 years, by highly controversial political policy, and by profound social change. This was the first change of administration under conditions of modern Big Government—the first since the American government found itself with accepted broad welfare and economic responsibility on the domestic scene and with major power responsibilities in a divided and warring world. Since the last full change, the size of the federal civil service had increased over 400 per cent, governmental expenditures over 16 fold.[4]

Extravagant campaign slogans to throw the rascals out, eliminate corruption, economize, and put through a major

---

[3] Jay Walz, "Help Wanted: Top Men for Washington," *New York Times Magazine* (Oct. 13, 1957), p. 24.

[4] Herman M. Somers, "The Federal Bureaucracy and the Change of Administration," *American Political Science Review,* Vol. 48 (March 1954), p. 131.

housecleaning were among the dominant themes of the campaign and were taken with utmost seriousness by highly placed business executives who supported the Republican cause. As Somers suggests:

> There is ample evidence that Candidate and President-elect Eisenhower and many of his leading supporters genuinely believed that the executive branch had become contaminated with grafters, incompetents, political hacks, "socialistic thinkers," and even a not inconsiderable number of disloyal persons, and that a wholesale substitution of honest men with administrative ability would solve most of our problems. The administrative talent would have to be found in men with a different social orientation than that which presumably had dominated the executive branch during the two previous decades.[5]

Fortune, a leading magazine for business executives, observed the advent of the new administration in a characteristic vein:

> When Mr. Eisenhower's brisk businessmen move into their Washington offices this month, they will not find themselves surrounded entirely by friends, or all the corridors ringing with camaraderie. There will still be a lot of people around who view businessmen with a fishy eye. Such highly placed Fair Dealers as Oscar Chapman and Oscar Ewing will have departed, of course, but a legion of little Oscars will still be on or in the bureaucratic anthills, enjoying long-term appointive jobs or perched out of reach in civil service. . . .
>
> The problem is not competence. Many are very competent. The problem they present revolves around their

[5] *Ibid.,* p. 131.

ideology. They are in key positions. For no matter what is said about the nonpolitical nature of civil-service appointments, in twenty years of Roosevelt and Truman it has been the dedicated New and Fair Dealers who have floated to the top. American businessmen have a long bill of particulars against this legion of little Oscars.[6]

Again, in its portrait of Gulliver, the businessman in Washington during the Korean War, *Fortune* captured the feeling of the new executive in a bewildering environment:

> After he gets the big hello at the White House, and a few kind words from Wilson, or Eric Johnston, or whomever, he rides off to the battleground, where his deflation begins. There he will meet his "administrative officer," a man whose name he has never heard before upon whom Gulliver will find himself, in the first few weeks, painfully dependent.[7]

Political executives who assumed direction of governmental agencies in 1953 and after usually had a profound distrust of the bureaucracy they inherited, especially the top career officials. The latter, scarcely any of whom had ever experienced a change of political party control in Washington, were uncertain, and, in some cases, fearful and wary. Unable to communicate with the bureaucracy and spurred by the desire to make good on inflated campaign promises, many of the Eisenhower executives were subject to early frustration. They needed, among other things, an orientation toward their new roles based on a reasoned understanding of the political environment. They

[6] "The Little Oscars and Civil Service," *Fortune* (January 1953), p. 77.
[7] Robert Sheehan, "Gulliver Goes to Washington," *Fortune* (June 1951), pp. 102-03.

desperately needed a usable explanation of the way in
which the political process operates.

THE APPOINTEE'S PROBLEMS OF ADJUSTMENT

With the experience of the change in executive leadership in 1953 clearly in mind, the Round Table turned its attention to the adjustment problems faced by an executive
during the first few months on the job and those faced by
career staffs in their relations with new bosses.

Importance of Previous Experience.   A career executive,
reflecting on the adjustment of the top executives in his
department during their early weeks on the job, recalled:

> With regard to the first six months' experience, the
> situation in the department was perhaps novel. Our three
> new top men were very knowledgeable fellows even
> though they had never held that kind of position before;
> in one way or another, they had learned a great deal about
> the affairs of Washington. So we had an operating team
> from the very first week. Their previous experience was
> obtained through service on policy and advisory commit-
> tees, in military service, and in private associations like
> the Committee for Economic Development. Some of the
> department's most important decisions of the first Eisen-
> hower term were made during the first three weeks.
>
> Our situation was also helped considerably by the exist-
> ence of good relations between the incoming secretary and
> the outgoing group. Consequently, there was mutual respect
> and confidence between the groups and good communica-
> tion. The outgoing executives wanted to help orient the
> new secretary and his staff and the new executives were
> prepared to be helped. There was a chance for some good

staff work. In the end we had a very smooth transition, mainly because we had a business-oriented group going out and a business-oriented group coming in. They understood each other.

A former federal executive commented:

I think we will find that secretaries and assistant secretaries who can trace their governmental connections back to service on the Business Advisory Council of the Commerce Department and the Committee for Economic Development and similar groups have been trained to think in terms of public policy. My guess would be that these people have been relatively more successful than those businessmen who lack such experience.

Another career executive reported a significantly different experience in the adjustment of new executives:

This is an area in which generalization may be impossible. The various men appointed by the President to top executive posts in Washington come from varying backgrounds; they have entirely different views about government and their roles in government. In my department in the past few years, we have had many types of assistant secretaries. One assistant secretary was a member of the Young Republicans for Eisenhower in New York State and very active politically. He was oriented in the direction of attempting to achieve the most for the President and his political party in program development in the shortest possible time. He showed tremendous interest in his job.

In contrast, we had another assistant secretary who was not oriented politically in any way. He had to start from the ground up in making political contacts. He stayed on the job only about one year. His successor, who stayed for two years, was much more active politically and knew his way around Washington like a veteran. He had more contacts than you could shake a stick at. Although he was a strong supporter of the President, he regarded himself as a maverick in politics. He had many friends on the Democratic side and was able to resist many of the approaches of the Republican party.

As I review the record of the various assistant secretaries, I see a wide variation in their ability to orient themselves to their jobs. By and large, lawyers have oriented themselves faster than businessmen. They seem to be able to grasp the nature of the job of the federal executive more rapidly. Some educators, especially those with some previous governmental experience, usually adapt themselves more quickly than most businessmen.

Some previous contact with the federal government, such as military service has a major impact on adjustment to the political and administrative aspects of government:

Even a man who has served in the armed forces in Washington brings to his new job a sensitivity which other men simply have not acquired. The optimum experience is probably participation somewhere in the federal hierarchy, military, if nothing else. This gives a man an awareness of the federal environment that he cannot get any other way. Unless he has this combat experience, he is not worth much to the government.

Orientation on the Job. A political executive with several years' service in the Administration reported on his situation:

This discussion has been extremely interesting to me because various departments have differed in the type of people brought into executive positions. My department brought in only businessmen, but we have not had very great turnover in these jobs. As an assistant secretary I started without a ready-made organization, while the other assistant secretaries inherited going organizations and staffs. I had to find career people to make up a staff. Just as it is in business, people have a great respect for you if you pick them out and hire them. They think your judgment is very good. So it is easier for a new executive to influence his career staff if he is setting up his own organization instead of maintaining an existing one. On the other hand, starting a new organization is very tough. It would have been easier if some skeleton of an organization at least had existed.

I think the impression that hit me the hardest during the first few months on the job was the complete lack of an orientation and indoctrination program for new assistant secretaries. Some departments have now organized some kind of orientation plan, but my department had nothing. The new men just came in and there you were. In business, now, the new executive would have been told much more about the job and the environment. We have talked here about the kinds of things that a new man must learn. For instance, everything a federal executive does impinges upon the authority of another agency. You are not free in personnel matters because of the authority of the Civil Service Commission. The Bureau of the Budget and the General Accounting Office limit your spending powers. Everything you do affects other people so much more than in business. You are not free to act, and it takes time to learn how to get along. In government, you need a lot more lead time to accomplish something significant. It is quite easy to become bitter and frustrated early in the game and say frankly, "To hell with it." I was tempted more than once to do exactly that, but I am glad to say that I didn't.

A political executive in a large department described his reactions during his first few months on the job:

I am impressed with how the new assistant secretary comes into his department of perhaps 50,000 people and finds that the secretary is able to appoint only about 100 of them. Even though I was able to appoint an assistant of my own selection, I naturally wondered whether the civil service staff that surrounded me would support the policies of the secretary and whether they were going to be hostile. There was a period of several months in which I tried to feel them out to see whether I was going to be able to be perfectly at home with them.

There is, however, a broader difficulty in getting acclimated to a new job, and that is the ability to grasp the public interest character of problems and issues that one must deal with. In government, the executive has to learn to measure his ideas on what public interest is at stake against the views of other agencies. Coming from business, I would say that this is the most difficult thing of all. In business, if you give an order, it is executed. You may talk to one or two people about it, and it is done. But that certainly is not true in Washington.

A new under secretary described his current situation:

I have been on the job about four weeks now. Three or four of us were appointed at the same time, so we have had an orientation program for the group as a whole. It has been very valuable. At the same time, before our orientation had been completed, we began to operate. We attended meetings where we were expected to state the department's position. The formal orientation had to be pushed aside because of the pressure of operating problems.

I have served as an executive in several different posts and environments. I think it is the better part of wisdom for the political executive to put himself in the hands of the career people. I like to find an old-time secretary on the ground and an administrative assistant who knows his way around, and use them to become better acquainted in Washington. Then I try to listen in order to learn faster. I ask questions. At the same time, it is important to be careful not to become the captive of other people.

The federal government is so vast that it is hard to generalize about the early experience of new executives. I have a feeling that the group of executives that have just come into our department are pretty much the same sort of fellows. I think that our greatest difficulty is not adjustment to one another or to the career staff but rather to the other departments and agencies and to Congress. There is the area where the new executive is likely to be most baffled by Washington. I find nothing in my previous experience in two state governments that helps me to understand the relationship of the executive with Congress and other agencies.

Another difficulty in my department, which is relatively new and where the turnover in executive positions has been fairly rapid, is that the top jobs are still rather fluid. The new man can make out of the job whatever he wants. It is not neatly structured and laid out. No man has yet held one of these jobs long enough to give it clarity and precision in the definition of duties and responsibilities. Another reason, perhaps, why the jobs of the assistant secretaries are still very flexible is that they are in essence not line jobs but staff posts involving coordination of the various operating agencies in the department. This type of job is harder to establish firmly than the line job.

However difficult the adjustment of a new departmental executive may be, the case of executives in nondepartmental agencies is probably more problematical. As one career executive stated:

Most of us in the Round Table are located in departments where we have a fairly clear line of command that goes right up to the President. We have some assurance that some attention will be given at the top to the problems that we raise. But the executives I am really worried about are those who don't have any line of command to the top. They get appointed to a job, are kicked off the back of the boat, and told to swim. I mean such agencies as the Federal Civil Defense Administration, the Housing and Home Finance Agency, and the Small Business Administration. Sometimes the problem is serious in the service agencies like the Civil Service Commission or the General Services Administration. In these agencies, there is an entirely different atmosphere from the kind that surrounds the cabinet and subcabinet group of executives. The job of orientation is probably more difficult for these men.

Getting Acquainted with Career Executives. While recognizing the natural tendency of the new political executive to be very skeptical in his attitude toward the career staff, the Round Table warned sharply against too much distrust. One career executive stated:

The new political executive needs to realize that the career staff is also skeptical of him. In order to overcome the latent hostility or diffidence of the career staff, the political executive needs to take some initiative in getting acquainted with it. He must at least take the trouble of letting the people who have been around for some time talk to him. For most of them, it is necessary to learn a new vocabulary. As one cabinet officer told me: "I had to learn how to understand problems in somebody else's language. That is something I have never had to do before." There is an unfortunate tendency for political executives to carry their suspicions beyond a useful point. At least they should not be reluctant to talk to their career staffs. The problem is undoubtedly more difficult in a change of administration and especially when political control moves from one party to another. But the problem is with us all of the time.

REACTIONS OF CAREER STAFFS
TO POLITICAL APPOINTEES

At the same time, the transition period calls for a more understanding attitude on the part of career officials. The situation in 1953 was in some ways more extreme than in the previous transitions in this century involving party overturn: those of 1913, 1921, and 1933. The need for mutual understanding was even greater. As a career executive explained:

The deep mistrust by the incoming political appointees of the career people stems from a variety of factors. We had a change of administration after 20 years, which was a long dry spell for the Republican party. During the thirties we had a social and economic revolution for which the Republicans blamed the Democrats and for much of which the Democrats were willing to take credit. The changes during this period were profound, and they were followed by both a World War and a "police action," both of which by 1953 were being blamed on the Democrats. On top of that we had McCarthyism. All of these things came together in 1953 with the general effect of creating a tremendous question in the minds of the new administration about the reliability and in some cases even the basic loyalty of the civil service staffs. The year 1953 may have been so unusual as to rule out its use for purposes of generalizing about our orientation needs for new executives. The political executive ordinarily comes in with at least some suspicion and aloofness from the career staff, but I am convinced that it was unusually acute in 1953. The career staffs need not be "gun-shy" of all future changes on the basis of the 1953 experience.

A new political executive often feels that career officials regard him as an amateur in the administration of programs better left in their experienced hands. The career staffs, on the other hand, may be fearful of what the political executives may do to the programs they help to administer. They may take up defensive or holding positions, waiting for action by the new political executives.

What Career Executives Worry About.   The worries of a career executive were stated by one of them thus:

The shock of the 1953 change-over still hangs on four years later. I wonder if the political appointees sense that the top career officials have a natural psychological reaction, a sort of conditioned reflex that leads them to begin to cover up. The career executive wonders about "What kind of fellow do we have here? What does he think? Is he going to tear things apart, or does he understand what we have been doing around here?" A few may look upon the political executive as a passing phenomenon whose temporary presence and influence must be tolerated, but this is an extreme attitude that characterizes only a minority of them.

If a political executive leaves his walnut paneled offices and reaches down a couple of layers in the organization, he will find evidences of this concern and withdrawal. To put it plainly, the staff is scared. It is hard for the career guy to know whether the new political executive, in addition to all the other things he has to learn about his job, senses this situation. More than that, the career executive is deeply concerned about the reaction of the political executive. Will it be constructive or destructive? Will he turn to anyone for help or try to solve the problem himself? Or will he build up his own defenses and become really aggressive in defending himself against career people whom he now regards as hostile.

Another career executive cautioned against placing too much stress on the 1953 situation:

> We should not draw too many conclusions from this episode. The 1953 situation was unusual; there had been no such major change in the executive branch for 20 years. In my organization, for instance, there was not a single employee who, as a top level executive had ever gone through a change of political party control. None of the new political executives I deal with had been in the federal government before. Perhaps they were pretty starry-eyed until the day after the inauguration when they suddenly found that they had an immense department to run. They needed people who knew the ropes to help them, yet they distrusted those who could help the most.
>
> At the same time the career people distrusted the new executives because they didn't know just what was going to be done. They heard rumors, veiled threats of discharges, and so forth. What worried the career people more than anything else was this: would the new political executives have the facts before them before they made their decisions? We worried when we saw them turning to just one group of people to get their facts. We did not worry whether they would make the right decision if they had all the facts.

The Process of Mutual Adjustment. In the mutual adjustment of career and political executives, much depends on the kind of people they are. They have to take each other on trust for awhile until they learn how far they can depend on one another. One participant stated that a career man can help his political boss a great deal by putting his job more or less on the line.

> I remember that I went to my new secretary and said: "I think a man coming into your job should have his own men around him. I am a career employee, but if you should decide to have your own man in this job, I hope you will first give me a trial because I think I can help you. But if you decide to have your own man, there will be no difficulty about it. All you need to do is tell me. If you want to try me first, I will attempt to give you all the facts bearing on your particular problem, and I will give them to you as accurately and impartially as I can. You will have to have faith in me until you learn to know me better. If you want me to make a recommendation, I will do so. If we get to the point where I cannot live with your decisions, I will get out. I will fight you outside the government, but I won't do so in the government. I won't make any end runs on you. Now, you don't know me from Adam, and you never heard of me before in all likelihood. You don't know whether I am going to live up to that statement or not. You will have to take it on faith." The secretary really needed me, but he didn't know it yet. As it turned out, we got along very well.

On the other hand, new political executives may not have a genuine opportunity to accept the offer of a career executive to resign. His dismissal might create a stormy reaction in the groups both within and outside the government interested in his programs. The career executive quoted above stated:

> I don't know how it would be with other agencies, but a lot of people might be very concerned if I resigned. I knew this, but the new secretary didn't know it yet, al-

though he would probably find it out very quickly. Nevertheless, I think my boss was entitled to a pledge of allegiance to support him. I think most career executives have customarily given it.

A political executive commented:

Most career executives have come up through the ranks. They have occupied a number of key jobs and have pretty broad experience. Many of them serve in stable programs that have developed by trial and error over several different administrations. In this situation, a new political executive, especially in a new administration, has grave problems orienting himself to the career service. A political executive probably serves in only one department in his career, and that experience will be totally different from anything else he has been through before. He has a great need for a pledge of allegiance from his career staff, but he also has a great need for these people to be such people that he can accept what they suggest.

One of his problems is that, with a new administration coming in, the whole election campaign has produced expectations of change that cannot possibly be effected. The campaign has been founded on the goal of tearing the whole place apart, policy, personnel, and everything else. The new executive finds out pretty soon that he cannot do what his natural inclination may be to do. Moreover, in an environment in which responsibility and authority are highly fragmented, the new executive strives to defend his position against presidential staffs, other agencies, congressional committees, and pressure groups. The political process seems to him to stress opposition and enmity rather than mutual respect and interdependency. It is not the kind of environment in which faith and trust are readily or easily placed in people one does not know.

Most career executives would like to help a political executive make the initial adjustment to government service as short and fruitful as possible. When asked what kind of orientation was most useful, a political executive responded:

If I had any more help, I wouldn't know what to do. I have listened to people and I have traveled over quite a lot of territory. I have read myself blind into the night. My advice to the career people is: Don't overdo it; don't be over-eager. There is a limit to what we can absorb in a short time. Go easy on the forced feeding.

A career executive concerned with personnel administration agreed:

This is a valid point. We made the same error in the Defense Department in 1953; we provided too much orientation. As a result the reception of our efforts by the political executives tended to sour after a while. It is better to ration it in small doses at the beginning and to continue it for long periods. Don't let it trail off. I don't know when the new executive finds his own depth and begins to operate under his own steam, but it is quite a while.

WANTED: AN ORIENTATION PROGRAM

The need for an orientation program for new political executives is almost universally recognized in Washington. Yet little has been done to develop one. As a career executive stated: "I have never found a single dissent among all the government people I talk to on the need for better orientation of new political executives to their jobs." A political executive agreed:

What I have been struggling for is some kind of in-doctrination that will give a new appointee half a chance to learn something useful about the government. A new executive cannot operate effectively in a going organization unless somebody has taken the trouble to show him the relationship of his job and agency to other agencies and how his job impinges on the prerogatives of others. It is easy to get overwhelmed with endless detail; I got that in my department. But what I missed and needed was the broad picture. It might be quite helpful if some of this indoctrination came from a nonpartisan or neutral source with a public orientation, like a research foundation.

A major problem in the development of orientation programs stems from the low status and prestige accorded government service in the United States and the derogatory attitude many Americans assume toward political commitment as such. A career executive formulated the problem as follows:

The attitude of some people toward the use of executives skilled in political affairs is very dangerous. To illustrate, I recently had a discussion with a cabinet officer about the desirability of appointing at a high level within a department a person who had, among other things, some political experience. I told him that the department needed more than any other single thing a person who was a skilled politician as well as an effective administrator. This comment went over like a lead balloon. The attitude was that there was some sort of irreconcilability between competence in terms of getting a job done and political skill and know-how. We have a basic problem of American customs here. We need to make people understand and accept the basic principle that political skill is something to be valued and respected and not something to be looked down upon as improper and unworthy of the consideration of serious, ethically-motivated people.

Unsuitability of the British Model. In its search for a model of orientation, the Round Table warned against the pitfall of looking longingly at the British political system for guidance.

It is not political skill that is looked down upon here as much as political commitment is feared. You ask a good deal of anyone to suggest trusting a major policy office to a man who has made a career in politics in a system in which there is no collective responsibility, particularly when his executive activity bears on his personal and individual political progress.

We look a lot at the things the British and other parliamentary regimes do. They are not and cannot be repeated here, because our political system is so fundamentally different with respect to the structure and exercise of political authority. Frankly we can never hope that American political parties will ever provide the kind of training for political jobs that the British do for the simple reason that in the United States there is no career in it. Here one cannot progress from assistant whip, to whip, to parliamentary under secretary, to deputy minister and eventually minister. There is no regular advance through the various political posts in control of the party apparatus.

What this means, in practical terms, is that the President's cabinet will almost always be composed of people who, as a group, are far from being the most influential persons in the President's party. Instead they are far more likely to be a new, extraneous and slightly inimical group which is introduced into the machinery of government by the President. They are people who, for the most part, need the help that an intelligent orientation program might provide. They need a lot more, but this at least is a bare minimum.

Two Types of Orientation.   In the opinion of the Round Table, two types of orientation are required. The first is primarily institutional indoctrination in the tradition, history, and activity of a particular department or agency. A career executive commented:

> If a new executive goes into the Treasury Department, he is going into a place vastly different from the Veterans Administration or the Department of Health, Education, and Welfare. He is coming into a department loaded with what we call tradition but which might more appropriately be termed bureaucratic habits and internal procedures. Each organizational unit has its own special environment. The term "tradition" dignifies it too much. It is more or less a system by which different parts of the same agency learn to tolerate each other. An orientation program in this area is needed to overcome the helplessness that a political appointee feels for a long period of time in dealing with an agency with a long history.

A former federal executive added:

> A new executive has to learn to understand the various groups and cliques with whom he deals. Unless he has this basic understanding, he will not be effective in the inevitable struggle for power in the agency. These struggles are by no means unique to government; there are plenty of them in universities and business. But they are strengthened in government by the vested interest of the government employee in his job. You get it especially in the military departments and agencies. For instance, it is un-

likely that any Secretary of the Treasury will make an appreciable impact on an agency like the Coast Guard. What the political executive must learn to understand is the political setting of his individual department.

A second type of orientation includes the broad political setting. One Round Table participant speculated:

> Department-by-department orientation is not ideal. It is a good start but not in itself adequate. It cannot quite fill the bill in explaining the intermeshing of various agencies and relationships with the Bureau of the Budget, GAO, and the Civil Service Commission. I wonder if the Executive Office might take the political appointee just as he enters the government and spend a few days with him before sending him on to the department. The Executive Office of the President ought to be able to give him a broader point of view and a positive attitude toward his job. In other words the first orientation in Washington might be presidential rather than departmental.
>
> This activity might be viewed by Congress with alarm as a form of brainwashing by the President, but it may gain acceptance.

Subsequent to the Round Table discussions, the President and the cabinet approved a proposal in August 1957 to establish a systematic plan for the orientation of newly appointed political executives. Under the plan each agency has been provided an outline of an orientation course, and each agency is instructed to give its new political appointees instruction in how the federal government operates. Some central direction from the White House has been provided to help develop and police the programs. While the plan has limitations, it significantly represents the first presidential recognition of the need for helping the new political executive to understand the complex federal environment and its impact on his job.[8]

Stages in the Life of the Executive.   The Round Table agreed that orientation programs would fill a real need if they could impart a sense of realism about Washington. In this connection a former executive in the defense mobilization program during the Korean war recalled the story of the four stages in the life of a qualified federal executive:

The first stage is that of the eager neophyte. The new appointee comes down on the plane, convinced that what Washington has badly needed is his ability to make crisp decisions and see problems clearly and realistically without any of the usual political overtones. He is going to apply this special skill, background, and experience he has acquired in the business world or elsewhere and things will rapidly become better. Once he is on the job, he appraises the problems confronting him, brings his high-powered brain to bear on them, and very gently makes some suggestions. To his dismay weeks go by and nothing very much happens.

Then he goes into what is called the frantic amoeba stage, in which he spins around much faster and a little more crisply. He advances from making oral suggestions to writing direct memoranda to the personnel involved. But he finds again to his dismay that there are people who do not agree with him. As a matter of fact, they seem to have a completely different point of view, and his proposals are finally rejected by the final arbiter in the matter.

He then goes into the mad bull stage. Now he thinks he ought to get acquainted better with his senator or his congressman, or he had better leapfrog the fellow who is

[8] See Rufus E. Miles, Jr., "The Orientation of Presidential Appointees," *Public Administration Review,* Vol. 18 (Winter 1958), pp. 1-6, 106-12.

directly above him and go to see the top man. He even considers whether he should not see some of the Washington columnists—Drew Pearson or the Alsop brothers.

Just before he takes the giant step, he realizes that after all he is not the head of the department. He may not even be the head of the bureau. So he goes into the fourth stage —the ancient Chinese mandarin stage, in which he is just going to look at the world, and do his own little job in his own simple way. No longer will he try to make over Washington or the government. He renounces the crusade to change everything completely. After being in this stage for a few weeks, he is suddenly called in by the big boss. Something he proposed in the neophyte phase has found great favor and is going to be put into effect. Again he takes on all the initial enthusiasm of the eager neophyte. That leads him successively to the frantic amoeba stage, the mad bull stage, and finally the Chinese mandarin stage. When he traverses all four stages in 24 hours, he has become a qualified executive.

This participant concluded:

If there were some way to tell on which side of the tree the moss is, and to get these political executives through that period of initial frustration without becoming soured, we might then get somewhere with orienting the political executive.

IX

Some Lessons of Experience

E ACH PRESIDENT of the United States faces the never-ending task of creating and replenishing a corps of officials to fill executive posts in more than three-score federal departments, agencies, boards, commissions, and corporations. As the Round Table participants recognized, the recruiting process must be based on a recognition that skills of business management are not readily transferable to government and qualities of high competence in business are not necessarily those that earmark the able government executive.

GOVERNMENT IS DIFFERENT

Early in the Eisenhower administration, it was clear to the new appointees that the environment of government differs markedly from that of private business, and that government makes exceptional demands upon executives. As George M. Humphrey, the first Republican Secretary of the Treasury in twenty years acknowledged:

> When I came to Washington in January [1953], I did not realize so clearly as I do now how different government is from business, and how much more difficult it is to get

things done. The job of making changes looked a lot easier from the outside.[1]

Factors that differentiate government from business apply to other aspects of American society as well. As the under secretary of agriculture in an earlier Democratic administration commented:

It is exceedingly difficult clearly to identify the factors which make government different from every other activity in society. Yet this difference is a fact and I believe it to be so big a difference that the dissimilarity between government and all other forms of social action is greater than any dissimilarity among those other forms themselves. Without a willingness to recognize this fact, no one can even begin to discuss public affairs to any good profit or serious purpose.[2]

Public Nature of the Government's Business. Above all else, government is differentiated from other activities by its public nature, which represents both its exposure to public scrutiny and its concern with the public interest. While the "public interest" perhaps has not been satisfactorily defined, it suggests that there are widely-shared interests in society that transcend those of an industry or a special group and that government exists in large part to promote and protect the interests of all the people. As the promoter of the public interest, government must be led and operated by men whose breadth of view and perspective are broader than those of a private individual intent on gaining personal profit. Understanding of the differences between government and other activities and insti-

[1] George M. Humphrey, with James C. Derieux, "It Looked Easier on the Outside," *Collier's*, Vol. 133 (April 2, 1954), p. 31.
[2] Paul H. Appleby, *Big Democracy* (1945), p. 1.

tutions requires recognition that no nongovernmental institution in society has such central and deep concern for everyone, is so closely connected to and dependent upon everyone, and carries on activities which are based so vitally on prevailing social values and reflect popular needs and aspirations.

Virtually nothing that government does is immune from public debate, scrutiny, and inquiry. Matters of administrative detail that are private matters in business are often the subject of investigation and criticism.

> Each employee hired, each one demoted, transferred, or discharged, every efficiency rating, every assignment of responsibility, each change in administrative structure, each conversation, each letter, has to be thought about in terms of possible public agitation, investigation, or judgment. Everything has to be considered in terms of what any employee anywhere may make of it, for any employee may be building a file of things that could be made publicly embarrassing. Any employee who later may be discharged is a potentially powerful enemy, for he can reach the press and Congress with whatever charges his knothole perspective may have invited.[3]

Secretary Humphrey characterized the governmental situation similarly:

> In business it is usually easy to reply to incoming letters, and the replies can be pretty rough if the situation justifies. But in government! Any letter a Cabinet officer writes may at any time show up in the press, on the floors of Congress or in court. A government man must be certain his letter will stand up under the law, under public scrutiny and in the political forums. Every citizen who writes in

---

[3] *Ibid.*, p. 7.

is a constituent of two Senators and one Representative; practical politics requires them to act as his advocates, at least up to a point.[4]

The public nature of the government's business is characterized also by public accountability. Both in democratic theory and in practice, officials must be held accountable by law for the decisions they make, the things they do, and the money they spend. In the United States the objectives of maintaining close, continuous control over officials who exercise public power has ordinarily been achieved not by pinpointing responsibility for particular programs but principally by establishing limits to executive discretion and freedom of operation. Congress normally has surrounded executives with detailed rules governing the organizational structure of government offices, the hiring and firing of employees, the spending of money and accounting for its use, the purchase of office supplies, and the procedures and methods of public administration.

Restrictions on Executive Power. While the public may, from time to time, express its fear that government officials are too powerful, officials are likely to be impressed with the restrictions on their power. It may be a solace to embattled Republican executives in the Eisenhower administration that the following comment was made in 1945:

> Indeed, this sense of a lack of power is what drives people out of Washington. To have to "think of everything in terms of everything else" causes many men to think that they are so hedged about by restrictions that they "can't do anything," with the result that, after a while, they simply give up with a feeling that they might as well

---

[4] Humphrey, *op. cit.*, p. 31.

go back home. The orders and statutes in our big democracy do not invest persons with power; they invest organizations with responsibility.[5]

Scope of Governmental Programs. Another characteristic that differentiates government from all other institutions and activities is the breadth of its activities and their pervasive impact on individuals and groups. American government helps to support the destitute, the blind, and the dependent. It sponsors youth clubs to eliminate juvenile delinquency and promotes agricultural development. It inspects meat and insures home loans, bank deposits, and human lives. It operates railroads, plans and constructs highways, generates and sells electric power, and subsidizes ships, airlines, and the newspaper industry. It mediates disputes between labor and management, runs employment offices, and guarantees workers the right to join a union of their own choosing. It clears slums and subsidizes low-cost housing. It makes payments to farmers for soil-conserving practices and warehouses surplus food. It provides tariff aid to domestic industry, free medical care for veterans, economic data for businessmen, and navigation aids for shippers.

Since the basic change in international affairs and the resulting reorientation of American foreign policy in the 1940's, national security and international politics have become more and more significant in public affairs. Military and defense activities and the conduct of foreign affairs account for more than half of the expenditures of the federal government. Today national security involves not only the training of combat soldiers, but also the education of the nation's youth, and the continued development of scien-

[5] Appleby, *op. cit.,* p. 38.

tific facilities for research in atomic energy, cosmic rays, ballistic missiles, jet aircraft, and other subjects. In emergency periods, national security may require mobilization of the nation's economy and manpower for concentration on the tasks of war or defense.

Since the depression of the 1930's, the facts of economic life and the political realities of the modern industrial world have compelled government to accept primary responsibility for the satisfactory operation of the domestic economy. Public opinion no longer tolerates severe economic depressions, and in an economic crisis no administration can avoid remedial governmental action. As President Eisenhower said in 1956:

> Experience . . . over many years has gradually led the American people to broaden their concept of government. Today we believe as strongly in economic progress through free and competitive enterprise as our fathers did, and we resent as they did any unnecessary intrusion of government into private affairs. But we have also come to believe that progress need not proceed as irregularly as in the past, and that the Federal Government has the capacity to moderate economic fluctuations without becoming a dominant factor in our economy.[6]

Size and Complexity. The federal government is the largest employer and most complex enterprise in the country. In January 1958, about 2.4 million civilians were employed full-time while personnel on active military duty numbered about 2.8 million. In contrast, the American Telephone and Telegraph Company, the nation's largest private employer, had 800,000 employees, and only four

[6] *Economic Report of the President,* Transmitted to the Congress January 24, 1956 (1956), p. 10.

other American corporations had as many as 200,000 workers: General Motors, with about 600,000; General Electric, with about 280,000; United States Steel, with about 260,000; and the Great Atlantic and Pacific Tea Company, with about 200,000.[7]

Many federal departments and agencies are as large as most big corporations. In June 1958, civilian employment exceeded 50,000 in ten departments and agencies: Post Office, 538,000; Army 416,000; Navy, 364,000; Air Force, 316,000; Veterans Administration, 172,000; Agriculture, 101,000; Treasury, 77,000; Commerce, 57,000; Interior, 56,000; and Health, Education, and Welfare, 55,000.[8] According to the Hoover Commission Task Force on Personnel and Civil Service, in 1954 there were about 350 major operating bureaus below the departmental and agency level, and 65 separate departments, agencies, boards, commissions, and corporations. The median size bureau among the 266 bureaus studied in detail by the Task Force was 1,800 people. Forty-four had more than 5,000.[9]

The size of the governmental establishment has contributed to its extraordinary complexity. Government activities have grown in piecemeal fashion in response to the demands of a dynamic society, and administrative authority has been dispersed widely and at times chaotically through several layers of administration. Important matters are rarely the exclusive concern of a single bureau or agency. The decisions of one agency affect, and are affected by the

[7] Paul T. David and Ross Pollock, *Executives for Government* (1957), p. 2.
[8] U.S. Civil Service Commission, *Monthly Report of Federal Employment* (June 1958), Table I, pp. 4-5.
[9] U.S. Commission on Organization of the Executive Branch of the Government, *Task Force Report on Personnel and Civil Service* (1955), p. 201.

decisions and programs of other agencies. This interpenetration of governmental activities makes it necessary for an executive to share powers of decision with others. He rarely has final authority, and his authority is rarely commensurate with his responsibility. It is not possible to organize the executive branch so that each department, bureau, or agency has a full measure of independence and autonomy. Thus the need to provide co-ordinating devices is continuing and inescapable.

Interpenetration of Government Activities. Former Secretary Humphrey found the interpenetration of government activities to be the distinctive characteristic of government administration:

> Government is vast and diverse, like a hundred businesses all grouped under one name, but the various businesses of government are not integrated nor even directly related in fields of activity; and in government the executive management must operate under a system of divided authority . . . when a government executive decides on a course of action not already established under law, he must first check with other agencies to make certain his proposal does not conflict with or duplicate something being done by somebody else. It is common in government, much too common, for several agencies to be working on different facets of the same activity. The avoidance of overlapping or conflict calls for numerous conferences, for painstaking study of laws and directives, for working out plans in tedious detail so that what one Cabinet officer does will not bump into what another is doing—or run counter to our interests and activities abroad. . . .
>
> Before coming to Washington, I had not understood why there were so many conferences in government, and so much delay. Now I do. Everything is more complex. . . .[10]

[10] Humphrey, *op. cit.,* p. 31.

These factors impose a heavy burden on executives. As the Hoover Commission Task Force on Personnel and Civil Service asserted: "Because of the size, complexity, tempo, and interrelations of the Government's operations, the demand for competent managers has run ahead of the supply."[11]

Salary Differentials. Government executives are employed at salary levels well below those in private industry in roughly comparable positions. In all likelihood, government will never be able to reward its executives with salaries as high as those available in industry, and perhaps it never should. Nevertheless, existing wide discrepancies in executive salary levels deter promising men and women from pursuing careers in government, make it more difficult to keep able executives in government, and obstruct the interchange of executive personnel between private life and public service. Salary differentials would, however, be less significant if the prestige of government employment was greater. Not only must the government executive anticipate financial sacrifices, but he must also expect low prestige and considerable abuse and harassment from Congress and the public, who will occasionally question his integrity, the sincerity of his convictions, and his suitability for public employment.

INSECURITY AND INSTABILITY IN GOVERNMENT

The design of the American government tends to produce conflict, friction, and tension. Political power has been widely diffused on a geographical basis between the federal government and the states and within the federal govern-

---

[11] *Task Force Report on Personnel and Civil Service,* p. xxi.

ment itself among the legislative, executive, and judicial branches. What distinguishes the U.S. government from most other national governments is not the separation of powers but rather the degree to which that constitutional principle has been modified drastically by devices of checks and balances.

> . . . everybody who has observed American government in action knows that much of the tumult and the shouting derives from the fact that virtually all *power is shared* between rival units of government driven by different interests. What the founding fathers designed was a system of relatively discrete areas of responsibility—the President as the executive and the Congress as the legislature, each politically independent of the other. But there is in reality no completely clean division between execution and legislation and the so-called "checks" furnished by the Constitution are, in fact, forms of shared power.[12]

Fragmentation of Political Power. The fragmentation of political power by the proliferation of checks and balances has made legislative-executive relations a source of built-in conflict in the federal government. Just as the sprawling executive branch was put together by bits and pieces, so Congress is composed of a series of small legislatures—the committees—where the real legislative power is exercised. The party system, in turn, is anchored in state and local political organizations whose concern for local and sectional interests takes precedence, normally, over national issues of public policy. Interest groups, in turn, try to perpetuate the dispersion of political power because

[12] Herman Miles Somers, "The President, the Congress, and the Federal Government Service," The American Assembly, *The Federal Government Service: Its Character, Prestige, and Problems* (1954), p. 53. Italics in the original.

the lack of some central control within the federal government increases their capacity to influence operations. In such a setting, a high premium has been placed on the unifying influence of the President.

The survival of individual agencies as effective administrative organizations in this environment depends substantially on the ability of executives to operate in an atmosphere of friction and tension and to stabilize that environment by collaborating with congressional committees, interest groups, and other sources of political support. At the same time, however, the building of defensive alliances in the departments and agencies strengthens the drive for operating autonomy and makes the presidential task of political and administrative integration more difficult. As one member of the Round Table stated:

> The instability of the political environment in Washington is a direct function of the presidential system. It is set up to produce conflicts. While the conflicts may not necessarily touch an executive directly, they certainly determine the environment in which he works. Even in days when the administration seemed most completely in control of Congress, there was a great deal of backbiting and pulling and hauling. The place was far from tranquil even in those days. Executives in Britain have their trials and tribulations, but everything there is better cushioned and more neatly ordered. The trials are just as great, but the corners are not as sharp. The executive is more apt to be bruised than cut to pieces.

In the American political system, powerful centrifugal forces and tendencies infinitely complicate the art and process of governing. For better or worse, the splintering of authority and responsibility in the federal government has established limits to effective administration that can be overcome only by political leadership and popular approval. As the experience of former Secretary of the Army Robert Stevens indicates: "The security of a family textile business is not good training for an alley fight."[13]

Consequences of Democracy. Apart from the constitutional and structural factors that contribute to the instability of the federal environment, other institutional arrangements, values, and attitudes, more or less indigenous to democratic government, produce a sense of insecurity in government executives. According to one Round Table participant: "A democratic society has a thousand ways of making its rulers insecure, and we presumably don't want to change very many of them. Even the elected official runs scared, and that is the way we want him to run."

The imperatives of democratic government call for a multitude of rules governing routine administrative operations as well as some devices designed to limit the discretionary authority of executives in making large decisions. For the sake of public accountability, executives in government are required to live in a goldfish bowl, with Congress, the interest groups, and the press watching all the time.

Although it is difficult to account for precisely, a sense of personal insecurity seems to be a characteristic of executive jobs in Washington. The environment in which public business takes place seems to raise the issue of whether an executive is doing anything useful in his job or whether he is wanted or needed. One executive described it as:

> . . . the sort of feeling all the time that you have to stop to reassess your relationship to the job and your contribution. You ask yourself: Are you really needed? Are you

[13] Arthur Moore, "Why Businessmen Are Leaving Washington," *Harper's Magazine* (September 1954), p. 28.

really wanted? There is a sense also of responsibility to the job and a questioning whether you are measuring up to it. This is a terribly pervasive feeling. It motivates a great deal of what most of us do.

Business executives probably suffer from tensions that may not be distinguishable from those of government executives. But according to one participant with extensive executive experience in both government and private business:

> This operation in a goldfish bowl does seem to make the tensions of the public service much greater than those I see in business. In business you can delegate to a greater degree and hold people down the line responsible. In government the focus of responsibility on the top executives is much greater than in the corporations I have worked with.

The diffusion and sharing of power in American politics tend to make every government organization pluralistic in its interests, while most business corporations are monolithic in their organization. Consequently, the executive in government is limited in the possibilities of large-scale delegation of authority.

While tensions may be acute in business, they tend to concern matters that are less fundamental than those that preoccupy many executives in government. One participant observed:

> The man who makes a mistake in the shoe manufacturing business by picking the wrong styles can measure his judgment in terms of the volume of sales. He may be able to recover his financial losses next year. In any case, after all, it is his money, and you can't take that with you. But the fellow in a bureau of the Atomic Energy Com-

mission deals with the survival of the country and even the fate of mankind. His job accomplishments cannot be calculated neatly and objectively. He feels a kind of wearing responsibility that few business executives feel. The consequences of error are so catastrophic and irreparable that sober and serious fellows would feel worse in administering that responsibility than they would in making financial decisions.

The Round Table concurred with the conclusion of the Hoover Task Force on Personnel and Civil Service that the heart of the federal personnel problem lies in increasing the supply of executives available within the government on a stable basis. The problem has been difficult to solve because the capacities which are so essential in government executives are nowhere systematically developed in American life. As the Task Force stated: "To lead the life of a political executive of high rank amidst the asperities of American politics is a test of toughness, of intelligence, and of devotion to the public interest."[14]

Although the Task Force referred only to politically appointed executives in the passage quoted, the observations are applicable to high ranking civil service executives as well.

SATISFACTIONS DERIVED FROM THE JOB

In its discussions of the jobs of federal executives, the Round Table talked frankly and spontaneously about such matters as the political setting of executive work, the executive's relationship to Congress, the jobs and skills of career executives contrasted with those of political

[14] *Task Force Report on Personnel and Civil Service,* p. 40.

executives, and the limitations on executive discretion in the federal government. Throughout its talks, the Round Table tended to emphasize, as noted in Chapter I, the problems faced by federal executives. It hoped that thoughtful discussion of the factors that make it difficult "to get things done" in Washington might encourage other executives to face up to complicated and difficult issues in the management of various programs and activities of the federal government.

When members of the Round Table were given an opportunity to review their extended comments about federal executives, a question was raised whether the discussions stressed too much the frustrations of the job. The consensus of the Round Table was that pessimism was not the quality that earmarked their discussions.

> What we have been doing is trying to face up realistically to some difficult problems. We have tried to describe an extremely difficult, complex, and, at times, frustrating job. But every important job is frustrating at times. If, for a fleeting moment, we wonder if we have exaggerated certain aspects of our jobs, it helps to recall that all important jobs have elements of complexity and frustration.

The Round Table hoped that a report of its conversations might be helpful to a new executive if it could account for the disappointments he would encounter in his government service. As one member stated: "There are going to be some things that he can't do anything about. But if he understands that other people are having the same troubles, it will be immensely easier for him to bear up under it. And if he is forewarned, he will be better prepared."

A member who subsequently retired from government service expressed the Round Table's views clearly:

We must be careful to maintain a realistic outlook toward our jobs. Government employment today should be painted as it is without gloss. All of us who are in government as teachers, civil servants, and policy people have a liking for affairs of state. We are people of generally good intentions who want to do good through the state and promote the well being of society. Therefore, after taking a realistic look at the employment situation in government, our inherent idealism comes to the fore, and we want to brighten up the picture a little. This picture could certainly be a happier one, but let us be sure to make it so by plumbing the present deficiencies and overcoming them rather than by concealing any factors that may make government service less appealing.

While the Round Table resisted the temptation to sugar-coat the job of the federal executive, it did try to indicate why its members stayed on the job, despite the complexities and obstacles encountered in Washington. One member asked: "Are there any of us who can think of something we would rather do because it would be more satisfying than what we do now?" A participant with many years of experience as a business executive prior to his government service said:

I look over my long experience in business before I came to Washington and contrast it with my government service. I conclude that this is one of the most satisfying experiences I have had. Even though there are frustrations and disappointments in dealing with other executive agencies and with Congress, I still wouldn't trade my present job for one in business. I would not trade because in the end, through our methods of give and take, we arrive at something that may not be perfection but it usually does get us on the road toward a better way of life. Compromise is something I didn't know before I came here, at least in the same degree. I learned that compromise is vitally important in government and society. This is a lesson that more Americans need to learn. Many of us come into government with a fixed and simple picture of government operations only to learn, if we stay for more than a few months, that things can't be done here as they are handled in a single company by a president and his board of directors.

A former government executive added:

When I went back to the clubs I was going to before, I found that people were talking about the same things they were when I left four years before. They seemed to have no conception of what the government was or how it worked. I felt like I was back in a little boy's game, despite the fact that I was making five times as much money as I did in Washington.

One participant was emphatic in his strong endorsement of executive work in government:

The privilege of executive experience in the federal government is strongly affirmative. The daily involvement in critical programs affecting large numbers of people offers a stimulation that cannot be equalled in other types of executive positions. Even the conflicts and pressures in the job offer an exciting "gamesmanship" experience for every executive. The association with other Americans from all segments of the community in a common program contributes significantly to personal development and understanding. Success, even in a limited area, becomes more meaningful because of the process through which it has been achieved and because of the broad impact of its consequences. Although demanding, such an experience is also rewarding. Few men or women are able to duplicate the positive quality of such an experience outside the government.

The Round Table's views on the rewards of federal executive life were substantiated by a number of former executives who had served in subcabinet and similar positions in recent years. One wrote:

I have been out of government service three years, and it is difficult to generalize because there are so many contradictions, but here goes:

1. It was the most interesting and satisfactory working experience I have had. I enjoyed the feeling of contributing to big things and to some extent of having made a useful personal contribution.

2. Personal associations within the government, being much less competitive, are more friendly and enjoyable. I felt a community of purpose with people I liked very much.

3. I stayed about long enough. Disposing of other people's money, necessary though it is, is not the same as earning it.

4. My personal affairs are now nearly back to where they were before I went to Washington.

5. I would do it again.

Another former executive wrote:

I consider the time I spent in Washington as the most stimulating assignment I have ever had. Having been quite critical of certain government trends in Washington while in business, I was challenged to find myself unexpectedly in a position where I could do something about the very things I had criticized. It was a sobering experience. To exchange views with other government officials and to have one's convictions either sharpened or dulled proved to be a real policy-making test. I don't begrudge for a moment the financial sacrifices I made. Working as a high government official was an honor I deeply appreciate.

A former assistant secretary now serving another branch of the government reflected soberly on his tour of duty in Washington:

A federal executive in Washington has rewarding but exasperating experiences. In the first place, he is called upon to work harder than he had imagined. One doesn't mind working from early in the morning to 7 or 7:30 p.m. six days a week for a period of several months or even a year or two. But after that time, I found myself longing for sunshine, a fishing pole, or a swimming pool. Another vexation is the inability to replace incompetent help because of seniority, "bumping rights," or veterans' preference. It should be easier to reward exceptional competence and easier to get rid of exceptional incompetence. Despite the gloomy tenor of these remarks, however, a tour of duty in Washington is a thrilling experience. One would not trade close association with present and past history for all the money in the world, nor would one want to do it permanently for the same compensation. The mere opportunity for contact, even though perhaps usually casual, with the country's leadership is satisfying to one's self-respect and constitutes adequate compensation to any man who wants above all else to be of some service to his country.

In thinking about the knowledge and understanding that new executives require and the political setting in which they work, the Round Table did not overlook those aspects that make government a unique human enterprise. Nor did it make light of the untidy, sprawling nature of the executive branch and the problems and pitfalls in attempting the essential task of bridging the constitutional gulf between the executive and legislative branches. Moreover, it had a fresh and realistic grasp of the environmental factors that make for instability in political life and provide wide-ranging opportunities to block, thwart, or dilute the decisions and policies of federal executives. Without sentimentality or superficial emotion, it was deeply convinced that service in an executive post in government can be immensely rewarding and satisfying.

SELECTED REFERENCES

Selected References

I. HISTORICAL BACKGROUND

Reeves, Floyd W. and Paul T. David. *Personnel Administration in the Federal Service.* Washington: U.S. Government Printing Office, 1937. 75 pp. (U.S. President's Committee on Administrative Management. Studies on Administrative Management in the Government of the United States, No. 1)

Describes the organization and character of federal personnel administration in the middle 1930's and outlines the development of a more satisfactory service of personnel administration in the federal government.

White, Leonard D. *The Jacksonians; A Study in Administrative History, 1829-1861.* New York: Macmillan Co., 1954. 593 pp.

A remarkable portrait of the state of the administrative art and an analysis of administrative developments in the national government in the period 1829-1860.

———. *Trends in Public Administration.* New York: McGraw-Hill Book Co., 1933. 365 pp.

Presents evidence of the increasing concentration of administrative power in the hands of the chief executive at all levels of government and the growing influence of business techniques and methods on governmental operations.

Wilson, Woodrow. *Congressional Government; A Study in American Politics.* Introduction by Walter Lippmann. New York: Meridian Books, Inc., 1956. 222 pp.

Written in 1883, this classic describes the role of Congress and the President, with emphasis on the diffusion of political responsibility and its implications for responsible democratic government.

II. GENERAL ENVIRONMENTAL FACTORS

Appleby, Paul H. *Big Democracy.* New York: Alfred A. Knopf, Inc., 1945. 197 pp.

Chapter 1 attempts to identify the "factors which make government different from every other activity in society." Chapter 2 considers the size and complexity of government administration.

————. "Formulating the Federal Government's Economic Program," A symposium. I. The Influence of the Political Order, *American Political Science Review,* Vol. 42, April 1948, pp. 272-83.

A perceptive article that sketches the political context of the process of developing the government's economic program.

Friedrich, Carl J. "Responsible Government Service under the American Constitution," Commission of Inquiry on Public Service Personnel, *Problems of the American Public Service.* New York: McGraw-Hill Book Co., 1935, pp. 3-74.

After noting the trend to more government service, this essay tackles the issue whether or not such service can be developed without destroying the American constitutional system in the process.

Graham, George A. "Personnel Practices in Business and Governmental Organizations," Commission of Inquiry on Public Service Personnel, *Problems of American Public Service.* New York: McGraw-Hill Book Co., 1935, pp. 337-431.

An attempt to test the hypothesis that methods of administration tend to be similar in business and governmental organizations of comparable size; it centers on the personnel problem of business and governmental organizations.

Hardin, Charles M. "Political Influence and Agricultural Research," *American Political Science Review,* Vol. 41, August 1947, pp. 668-86.

A study of the ways in which political influence has shaped the promotion of research policies and programs in agriculture.

Kaufman, Herbert. "The Growth of the Federal Personnel System," American Assembly, *The Federal Government Service: Its Character, Prestige, and Problems.* New York: Graduate School of Business, Columbia University, 1954, pp. 15-51.

An excellent anatomy of the federal civil service today and an historical account of how it got that way, with emphasis on the concept of neutrality and its meaning for the future of the federal service.

Morstein Marx, Fritz. *The Administrative State.* Chicago: University of Chicago Press, 1957. 202 pp.

An interesting study of bureaucracy in the modern world, including discussions of "the bureaucratic world" and "the making of career men."

Mosher, Frederick and Edith. "Distinguishing Marks of the Federal Government Service," American Assembly, *The Federal Government Service: Its Character, Prestige, and Problems*. New York: Graduate School of Business, Columbia University, 1954, pp. 113-79.

A clear statement of major significant differences today between the federal government service and business employment.

Sayre, Wallace S. "The Federal Government Service—A Possible Approach to the Topic," American Assembly, *The Federal Government Service: Its Character, Prestige, and Problems*. New York: Graduate School of Business, Columbia University, 1954, pp. 9-14.

A stimulating introduction to a volume on the federal government service today that poses the issue: "How can we combine, in the Federal Civil Service, high competence and high motivation with a system of control which insures the efficiency, responsiveness, and responsibility essential to a democratic society?"

Somers, Herman M. "The President, the Congress, and the Federal Government Service," American Assembly, *The Federal Government Service: Its Character, Prestige, and Problems*. New York: Graduate School of Business, Columbia University, 1954, pp. 52-80.

An examination of the issue: how and by whom should the federal government service be governed? With an emphasis on competition for control among the President, Congress, the courts, the majority political party, pressure groups, professional standards, and bureaucratic self-regulation.

Stein, Harold, ed. *Public Administration and Policy Development, A Case Book*. New York: Harcourt, Brace & Co., 1952. 860 pp.

Pp. X-XIX. An approach to public administration. A stimulating and perceptive introduction to the pioneering case book in public administration that sets forth various ways of approaching public administration and places administration in the context of politics.

U.S. Commission on Organization of the Executive Branch of the Government. *General Management of the Executive Branch*. Washington: U.S. Government Printing Office, 1949. 51 pp.

The general report of the first Hoover Commission em-

phasizing the need for greater presidential direction and co-ordination and ways to achieve them.

III. CONGRESSIONAL ASPECT OF THE ENVIRONMENT

Appleby, Paul H. *Big Democracy*. New York: Alfred A. Knopf,
Inc., 1945. 197 pp.
    Chapter 16 deals with the relationship between the execu-
tive and legislative branches, devoting considerable attention to
the problems of communication between the two branches.

Freeman, J. Leiper. "The Political Process: Executive Bureau—
Legislative Committee Relations." *Short Studies in Political
Science* No. 13. Garden City, N.Y.: Doubleday & Co., 1955.
72 pp.
    A study of relationships between key executive personnel at
the bureau level and leading members of congressional committees.

Gross, Bertram M. *The Legislative Struggle; A Study in Social
Combat*. New York: McGraw-Hill Book Co., 1953. 472 pp.
    Part II "Combat on the legislative terrain," 153ff. A
graphic, readable account of the process of legislative enactment.

Hyneman, Charles S. *Bureaucracy in a Democracy*. New York:
Harper & Bros., 1950. 579 pp.
    Part II. Six chapters devoted to a statement of the major
functions of Congress designed to direct and control the bureaucracy; by an author who favors a marked increase in the effectiveness of legislative supervision of the executive branch.

Key, V. O., Jr., "Legislative Control," Fritz Morstein Marx, ed.,
Elements of Public Administration. New York: Prentice-Hall,
Inc., 1946, pp. 339-62.
    A good, brief article on how Congress attempts to control
the bureaucracy.

Millett, John D. and Lindsay Rogers. "The Legislative Veto and
the Reorganization Act of 1939," *Public Administration Review*,
Vol. I, 1941.
    A case study in the development of an increasingly impor-
tant tool of legislative control over administration.

Truman, David B. *The Governmental Process; Political Interests
and Public Opinion*. New York: Alfred A. Knopf, Inc., 1951.
543 pp.
    Chaps. 11 and 12, pp. 321-394 discusses "The Dynamics
of Access in the Legislative Process" and "The Techniques of
Interest Groups in the Legislative Process."

White, William S. *Citadel: The Story of the U.S. Senate.* New York: Harper & Bros., 1956. 274 pp.

A sympathetic but perceptive account of the United States Senate.

IV. POLITICAL PARTY ASPECT OF THE ENVIRONMENT

Appleby, Paul H. *Big Democracy.* New York: Alfred A. Knopf, Inc., 1945. 197 pp.

Chapter 15. Points out that while adaptability and responsiveness to new national policies are necessary, wholesale turnover in personnel with changing administrations is neither possible nor practical. Civil service laws protect against arbitrary action but do not prevent changes that good administration may require.

Herring, E. Pendleton. *The Politics of Democracy; American Parties in Action.* New York: W. W. Norton & Co., 1940. 468 pp.

Chapters 4-14, 26. A provocative analysis of American politics that emphasizes the nature of the party system and its relations to other social processes. Emphasis on the extra legal implementation that helps make democracy work. Includes a discussion of patronage and the spoils system.

Key, V. O., Jr. *Politics, Parties, and Pressure Groups.* 4th ed. New York: Thomas Y. Crowell Co., 1958. 783 pp.

A leading textbook. See: Nature and Function of Party, pp. 218-49; Party Machine as Interest Group, pp. 381-405; Party Leadership in Legislation, pp. 702-41; Administration as Politics, pp. 742-64.

Macmahon, Arthur W. and John D. Millett. *Federal Administrators; A Biographical Approach to the Problem of Departmental Management.* New York: Columbia University Press, 1939. 524 pp.

The chapter, "Survival of Political Recruitment," pp. 439-46, describes six appointments, "clearly shaped by political considerations."

Mansfield, Harvey C. "Political Parties, Patronage, and the Federal Government Service," American Assembly, *The Federal Government Service: Its Character, Prestige, and Problems.* New York: Graduate School of Business, Columbia University, 1954, pp. 81-112.

Probably the best discussion of the dilemma of party patronage and the public service and analysis of the stakes of the President, Congress, and pressure groups in patronage.

V. INTEREST GROUP ASPECT OF THE ENVIRONMENT

Garceau, Oliver. *The Political Life of the American Medical Association.* Cambridge: Harvard University Press, 1941. 186 pp.

A fascinating account of perhaps the most effective and successful pressure group in the United States.

Kesselman, Louis C. *The Social Politics of FEPC: A Study in Reform Pressure Movements.* Chapel Hill: University of North Carolina Press, 1948. 253 pp.

A study of the movement for a permanent national Fair Employment Practice Commission, emphasizes the legislative battle.

Kile, Orville Merton. *The Farm Bureau Through Three Decades.* Baltimore: Waverly Press, 1948. 416 pp.

The story of the growth and development of one of the leading farm organizations and its influence on agricultural policy and administration.

Maass, Arthur. *Muddy Waters; The Army Engineers and the Nation's Rivers.* Introd. by Harold L. Ickes. Cambridge: Harvard University Press, 1951. 306 pp.

An evaluation of the impact of the Corps of Engineers on the development of the nation's rivers for navigation, flood control, and allied purposes, emphasizing the adjustment of group pressures. Contains case study of Kings River Project in Great Central Valley of California.

Truman, David B. *The Governmental Process: Political Interests and Public Opinion.* New York: Alfred A. Knopf, Inc., 1951. 543 pp.

Groups and Government: Introduction, pp. 45-65; Group Origins and Political Orientations, pp. 66-108; Interest Groups and Political Parties, pp. 262-87; The Dynamics of Access in the Legislative Process, pp. 321-51; Techniques of Interest Groups in the Legislative Process, pp. 352-94.

Probably the most stimulating contemporary treatment of the impact of interest groups on policy and administration.

VI. PRESIDENTIAL ASPECT OF THE ENVIRONMENT

Brownlow, Louis. *The President and the Presidency.* Chicago: Public Administration Service, 1949. 137 pp.

The author's first-hand knowledge and insight give special value to these lectures on the role of the President.

Graham, George A. *Morality in American Politics.* New York: Random House, 1952. 337 pp.

Chap. V, "The Executive," pp. 151-89. An interesting treatment of the role of the chief executive, the conflict between the President and Congress, and the obstacles in the way of achieving executive accountability.

Neustadt, Richard. "Presidency and Legislation: The Growth of Central Clearance," *American Political Science Review,* Vol. 48, 1954, pp. 641-71 and

———. "Presidency and Legislation: Planning the President's Program," *American Political Science Review,* Vol. 49, 1955, pp. 980-1021.

Best analysis of the legislative clearance function and the development of the President's legislative program.

Price, Don K. "Staffing the President," *American Political Science Review,* December 1946, Vol. 40, pp. 1154-68.

Considers problems of executive co-ordination and recommends development of an executive office secretariat.

Truman, David B. *The Governmental Process; Political Interests and Public Opinion.* New York: Alfred A. Knopf, Inc., 1951. 543 pp.

Chap. XIII, "The Ordeal of the Executive," describes "the play of interests throughout the executive's activity in legislation and discretionary administration." pp. 395-436.

VII. THE DEPARTMENTAL-BUREAU SYSTEM

Freeman, J. Leiper. "The Political Process: Executive Bureau—Legislative Committee Relations." *Short Studies in Political Science* No. 13. Garden City, N.Y.: Doubleday & Co., 1955. 72 pp.

A study of the relationships between key executive personnel at the bureau level and leading members of congressional committees.

Hensel, H. Struve and John D. Millett. "Departmental Management in Federal Administration; A Report with Recommendations." Washington: U. S. Government Printing Office, 1949. 60 pp. (U. S. Commission on Organization of the Executive Branch of the Government. *Task Force Report.* Appendix E.)

A study of the deficiencies of departmental management and a program for improving departmental management.

Hyneman, Charles S. *Bureaucracy in a Democracy.* New York: Harper & Bros., 1950. 579 pp. Direction and control within the administrative organization, pp. 421-97.

   A discussion of the role of the executive in federal government agencies by one who favors tight legislative control of the bureaucracy.

Leiserson, Avery. "Federal Executive Reorganization Re-examined." VI. Political Limitations on Executive Reorganization, *American Political Science Review,* February 1947, Vol. 47, pp. 68-84.

   An examination of the psychological, legal, and political considerations in the congressman's experience that predispose him to oppose executive reorganization and the differences between legislative and executive goals of reorganization.

Macmahon, Arthur W. and John D. Millett. *Federal Administrators; A Biographical Approach to the Problem of Departmental Management.* New York: Columbia University Press, 1939. 524 pp.

   Chapters 1-5, 16-17, 24. Organs of Leadership, pp. 3-151; a statement of the needs of departmental management and the principal ways in which these needs were met prior to 1939; and an examination of leadership at the bureau level.

Morstein Marx, Fritz. "The Departmental System," in his *Elements of Public Administration.* New York: Prentice-Hall, 1946. pp. 184-206.

   A good, brief statement of the departmental system in federal administration, including a picture of the business performed at the secretarial and bureau chief levels. Based mainly on World War II experience.

Truman, David B. *The Governmental Process; Political Interests and Public Opinion.* New York: Alfred A. Knopf, Inc., 1951. 543 pp.

   Chapter 14. This chapter deals with "The Web of Relationships in the Administrative Process," emphasizing the diffusion of leadership and multiple points of control within the executive branch.

VIII. THE JOB OF THE FEDERAL EXECUTIVE

Appleby, Paul H. *Big Democracy.* New York: Alfred A. Knopf, Inc., 1945. 197 pp.

   Considers the qualifications of the top executive in government (pp. 39-47); the importance of "operating on one's proper level" (pp. 65-77); the nature and importance of co-ordination (pp. 78-83) ; and basic principles in achieving administrative unity (pp. 84-96).

Caldes, William C. "Orientation of Presidential Appointees in the Department of Defense." *Personnel Administration,* January-February 1958, Vol. 21, pp. 32-37.

Corson, John J. *Executives for the Federal Service; A Program for Action in Time of Crisis.* New York: Columbia University Press, 1952. 91 pp.

    Asserts that the U. S. faces an executive crisis, *i.e.,* a failure to provide government with a system that gives it a fair share of the nation's best executive talent; the author examines the current demand for executives, how executives are hired and fired, and why men refuse to serve in executive posts in government; and recommends both short-run and long-term action to meet the demand for executive talent.

David, Paul T. and Ross Pollock. *Executives for Government.* Washington: The Brookings Institution, 1957. 186 pp.

    A timely discussion of central issues of federal personnel administration.

Harvard Business School Club of Washington, D.C. *Businessmen in Government: An Appraisal of Experience.* Washington: Harvard Business School Club of Washington, D.C., 1958. 44 pp.

    A study of the recruitment and performance of businessmen in executive positions in the federal government based on analysis of questionnaires completed by business executives and top-level career officials in government.

Lawton, Frederick J. "The Role of the Administrator in the Federal Government." *Public Administration Review,* Spring 1954, Vol. 14, pp. 112-18.

    A statement of the executive's job based on "personal experience in watching administrators in the conduct of administrative business."

Paget, Richard M. "Strengthening the Federal Career Executive." *Public Administration Review,* Spring 1957, Vol. 17, pp. 91-96.

Perkins, John A. "Staffing Democracy's Top Side." *Public Administration Review,* Winter 1957, Vol. 17, pp. 1-9.

Simon, Herbert and others. *Public Administration.* New York: Alfred A. Knopf, Inc., 1950. 582 pp.

    Chapters 18-19. Focuses upon "the struggle for existence" of government agencies, *i.e.,* "how organizations adjust themselves to the world about them; their relations with other and competing organizations, with Congress, and with the general public."

Somers, Herman M. "The Federal Bureaucracy and the Change of Administration." *American Political Science Review,* March 1954, Vol. 48, pp. 131-51.

One of the very few published articles attempting to analyze the effect of a change of national administration upon the federal service.

Spann, R. N. "Civil Servants in Washington: The Higher Civil Service and Its Future." *Political Studies,* February and October 1953, Vol. 1, pp. 143-61, 228-46.

Stone, Donald C. "Notes on the Governmental Executive: His Role and His Methods." *New Horizons in Public Administration; A Symposium.* University, Ala.: University of Alabama Press, 1945, pp. 44-69.

One man's view of the job of the federal executive, with emphasis on staff or non-operating functions.

————. "The Top Manager and His Environment," in Joseph E. McLean, ed., *The Public Service and University Education.* Princeton: Princeton University Press, 1949, pp. 51-69.

Brief statement of the environment of the federal executive that stresses the obstacles confronting the career executive in the federal government.

U. S. Commission on Organization of the Executive Branch of the Government (1953-55). Task Force on Personnel and Civil Service. *Report on Personnel and Civil Service.* Washington: U. S. Government Printing Office, 1955. 252 pp.

This report emphasizes the strengthening of top management by distinguishing between political executives and career administrators, improving large-scale employment practices, and strengthening the merit system. Contains full statement of the case for the senior civil service.

Walker, Robert A. and William A. Jump. "The Staff Officer as a Personality," *Public Administration Review,* Spring 1954, Vol. 14, pp. 233-46.

A brief biographical study of the influence and effectiveness of one of the foremost federal career administrators.

Young, John D. *Taking Over a New Executive Post.* Brussels, 1952. 26 pp. (International Institute of Administrative Sciences, Studies, No. 13).

Suggestions for a person who is about to take on a new executive post, especially on how he can obtain effective control of a new post.

INDEX

Index

Adams, Sherman, 145

Administration, change of, 31, 58, 60, 62, 91, 92, 119, 154, 178, 179, 187-8, 189, 190, 192

Agencies, federal, size compared with corporations, 206. *See also* names of.

Agency disputes, the case for, 28-30

Agricultural Extension Service, 79

Agricultural Research Service, 88

Agricultural Department, 67, 79, 88, 95, 128, 129, 130, 201, 206. *See also* Forest Service.

Air Force, 79, 206

American Legion, 76, 95, 131

American Telephone and Telegraph Company, 205

Appleby, Paul, 27n., 201n., 202n., 204n.

Army, 79, 81, 113, 206, 211

Army Engineers, 79, 81

Atomic Energy Commission, 109, 212

Atomic Energy, Joint Committee on, 109

British Ministry of Health, 44

Budget Bureau, 11, 20, 51, 66, 70, 72, 73, 76, 132, 147, 184, 197

Budget process, 20, 21, 50, 51, 72, 73, 100, 102

Bureau autonomy, causes of, 84

Business Advisory Council, 149, 182

Cabinet, Eisenhower use of, 68-9; need for orientation of, 195

Career executives. *See* Executives, career

Census Bureau, 88

Civil Service Commission, 50, 51, 70, 75, 76, 77, 78, 97, 184, 187, 197

Civil Service, Senior, proposal for, 40

Commerce Department, 29, 67, 79, 88, 128, 129, 149, 182, 206

Committee for Economic Development, 181, 182

Congress, 21, 22, 28, 32, 44, 45, 46, 52, 54, 56, 57, 58, 59, 61, 63, 72, 73, 74, 76, 77, 87, 90-119, 120, 127, 134, 135, 136, 154, 157, 186, 197, 202, 203, 208, 209, 211, 213, 215. *See also* Relationships, congressional; Time, executives with Congress.

Congressional committees, alliances of bureaus with, 84; Budget Bureau aid to agencies appearing before, 72; executives, appearances before, 86; executives relationship with, 109; resistance of bureaus to departmental controls sustained by, 86; time of political executive spent in hearings, 30; who can best represent agency before, 20-21

Co-ordination, presidential, 33-4, 65, 68, 70, 81-2, 118

Corson, John J., 138n., 147n., 150n.

David, Paul T., 39n., 138n., 152n., 206n.

Decision making, 19, 23, 34, 40, 43, 55, 56, 68, 110, 117

Defending agency programs, 22, 30, 37, 46, 86

Defense Department, 23, 25, 66, 67, 72, 99, 108, 158, 160, 193

Date Due

PRINTED IN U. S. A.